THE WORLD OF PAUL SLICKEY

by the same author

*

LOOK BACK IN ANGER
THE ENTERTAINER

*

with Anthony Creighton
EPITAPH FOR GEORGE DILLON

THE WORLD OF
PAUL SLICKEY

A Comedy of Manners

with Music

by

JOHN OSBORNE

FABER AND FABER

24 Russell Square

London

First published in mcmlix
by Faber and Faber Limited
24 Russell Square London W.C.1
Printed in Great Britain by
Latimer Trend & Co Ltd Plymouth
All rights reserved

All professional inquiries in regard to this play
should be addressed to the author's agent, Margery
Vosper Ltd., 53a Shaftesbury Avenue, London W.1.

No one has ever dedicated a string quartet to a donkey although books have been dedicated to critics. I dedicate this play to the liars and self-deceivers; to those who daily deal out treachery; to those who handle their professions as instruments of debasement; to those who, for a salary cheque and less, successfully betray my country; and those who will do it for no inducement at all. In this bleak time when such men have never had it so good, this entertainment is dedicated to their boredom, their incomprehension, their distaste. It would be a sad error to raise a smile from them. A donkey with ears that could listen would no longer be a donkey; but the day may come when he is left behind because the other animals have learned to hear.

CAST

in order of appearance

COPY-BOYS
TELEPHONIST
JO, *the Secretary*
JACK OAKHAM, *alias* PAUL SLICKEY
COMMON MAN
1ST NAVAL MAN
2ND NAVAL MAN
DEIRDRE RAWLEY
LADY MORTLAKE
TREWIN
MICHAEL RAWLEY
MRS. GILTEDGE-WHYTE
LORD MORTLAKE
SCHOOLGIRLS
GUIDE AND JOURNALIST
PHOTOGRAPHER
WENDOVER
GEORGE
LESLEY OAKHAM
FATHER EVILGREENE
EDNA FRANCIS-EVANS
CORNELIA TUESDAY
BELGRAVIA LUMLEY
IDA MERRICK
TERRY MAROON
SIX MEN JOURNALISTS
SIX LADY JOURNALISTS

The first performance in Great Britain of *The World of Paul Slickey* was given at the Pavilion Theatre, Bournemouth, on 14th April 1959. It was directed by the author. The music was by Christopher Whelen, the choreography by Kenneth MacMillan and the décor by Hugh Casson. The cast was as follows:

COPY-BOYS	David Harding
	Julian Bolt
JO, *the secretary*	Irene Hamilton
JACK OAKHAM, *alias* PAUL SLICKEY	Dennis Lotis
COMMON MAN	Ken Robson
1ST NAVAL MAN	Ben Aris
2ND NAVAL MAN	Geoffrey Webb
DEIRDRE RAWLEY	Maureen Quinney
LADY MORTLAKE	Marie Lohr
TREWIN	Aidan Turner
MICHAEL RAWLEY	Jack Watling
MRS. GILTEDGE-WHYTE	Janet Hamilton-Smith
GILLIAN GILTEDGE-WHYTE	Janet Gray
LORD MORTLAKE	Harry Welchman
LESLEY OAKHAM	Adrienne Corri
FATHER EVILGREENE	Philip Locke
GUIDE	Geoffrey Webb
1ST GIRL	Norma Dunbar
2ND GIRL	Pam Miller
3RD GIRL	Anna Sharkey
1ST MAN	Ken Robson
LADY PHOTOGRAPHER	Stella Claire
PHOTOGRAPHER	Charles Schuller

JOURNALIST	Geoffrey Webb
WENDOVER	Ben Aris
GEORGE	Tony Sympson
TERRY MAROON	Roy Sone

DANCERS:

Geoffrey Webb	Stella Claire
Ben Aris	Patricia Ashworth
Julian Bolt	Norma Dunbar
David Harding	Pam Miller
Ken Robson	Anna Sharkey
Charles Schuller	Jane Shore

TIME: THE PRESENT

The entire action of the play takes place between the office of Paul Slickey, Gossip Columnist for *The Daily Racket*, and Mortlake Hall, a stately home somewhere in England.

MUSICAL NUMBERS

ACT ONE

Don't think you can fool a Guy like me	Jack and Dancers
We'll be in the Desert and alone	Jack and Deirdre
It's a consideration we'd do well to bear in mind	Michael
Bring back the Axe	Mrs. Giltedge-Whyte
The Mechanics of Success	Guide and Journalists
Tell me later	Jack
The Income Tax Man	Lesley and Michael
Them	Jack and Dancers

ACT TWO

On Ice	Jo and Dancers
I want to hear about beautiful things	Mrs. Giltedge-Whyte
You can't get away with it	Father Evilgreene and Dancers
A Woman at the Weekend	Lesley, Jack, Deirdre and Michael
I'm hers	Terry
REPRISE: *I want to hear about beautiful things*	Mrs. Giltedge-Whyte
If I could be	Jack, Jo and Dancers

ACT I

SCENE ONE

The curtain goes up and a cloth covered in large keyholes is revealed, through which can be seen parts of the Paul Slickey office, and JO *sitting at his desk* U.L.

SIX LADY JOURNALISTS *and* SIX MEN JOURNALISTS *come on in front of the cloth and dance with newspapers.*

They end the dance and go through one of the keyholes R. *which is cut out. The last dancer curtseys, and goes through, the cloth goes away and the lights come up on the Offices of* The Daily Racket, *early Saturday morning.*

Upstage, C., *is a huge cloth representing a sheet of newsprint. In large letters all over is printed "Paul Slickey". The silhouette appears on the centre cloth of the man who is responsible for the Paul Slickey column. He wears a heavy, light-coloured overcoat, dark hat and bright brown shoes. When he is not embracing a* GIRL—*he uses a cigarette-holder. He turns and we see his profile for the first time. As we hear his voice, a linotype operator clatters out his words and pictures and words appear on the column as the silhouette walks away.*

VOICE: There were no moral fervours in London last night
(COPY-BOY *crosses from down* R. *to office desks where the dancers are sitting, and places galley-proofs on desks.*)
But it was good to welcome several glamorous examples of passionate bankruptcy in all kinds of places.
(*There is a chord from the orchestra.*)
Last night's events . . .
(*Orchestra chord. Photograph projected on to screen showing three typical Guards officers in civvies.*)

11

Last night's events . . .

(*Orchestra chord. Photograph of a regal lady in tiara bowing graciously from a Rolls Royce.*)

Last night's events . . .

(*Orchestra chord. Photograph of a bad-tempered-looking Bishop in gaiters, pushing aside a small boy.*)

Last night's events . . .

(*Orchestra chords. Three pigs at a party.*)

Last night's events were certainly a colourful milestone in the National Drive for organized triviality.

(*The projection fades out. Up* R. *a telephonist chants:* "Daily Racket. . . . Who? . . . Just a moment." *The phone rings in Slickey's office and* JO *picks it up.*)

JO: Who? . . . Jack Oakham . . . (*Stands*) Oh, it's you, sir. I'm afraid Mr. Oakham isn't here just at the moment. . . . Yes, sir, I will. . . . The moment he gets back.

(*She puts the phone back and reads from copy, standing downstage of the desk.*)

"As I walked away from the pageantry, the happy crowds, the faces of those loyal subjects, I stopped inside a shop doorway to light my pipe. And suddenly to my surprise, I saw shining on my cheeks, a small column of tears. Dot, dot, dot, dot." (*Sits on desk front.*) Well we've got one dot extra today. "I puffed hard and walked back to Fleet Street in the evening sunshine with a gay heart. There are times when it is good to be an Englishman."

(JACK OAKHAM, *alias* PAUL SLICKEY *enters from behind the screen and hangs his hat on the hatstand.*)

Oh, you've arrived! (*Goes to him.*)

JACK: I'm just going.

JO: Finished your copy? (*Picks up copy.*) Where have you been?

JACK: Getting loaded.

JO: The great man rang for you.

JACK: He did?

JO: From Bermuda. (*Hangs* JACK'S *coat on the stand.*)

JACK: So?

JO: (*admiringly*). You boys are so tough in this racket!
(COPY-BOY *enters from down* R. *and stands waiting for copy.* SECRETARY *hands it to him.*)
Here. They mustn't miss this one.
(*Exit* BOY *the same way.*)
Your wife left a message.

JACK: When?

JO: I don't remember. A few hours ago.

JACK: Oh, thank *you.*

JO: (*kisses him*). She says she's got some important clients from the Continent to see over the week-end, and will you go down to your father-in-law's on your own.

JACK: She must be still mad with me. (*To desk chair*)

JO: Don't tell me she's found out about you and that sister of hers!

JACK: No, it's not that. At least I hope not. She's still mad about that story I wrote about the Church Commissioners having invested money in her brassière company.

JO: Was it true?

JACK: What do you mean—true? Once you've said it in print, it's difficult to make it sound like a downright lie. You should know that by this time. It made a nice couple of columns. I simply suggested that the Church's one foundation might yet turn out to be an intimate undergarment in ear-pink and mystery-blue. Her old man was furious about it. Thank God, he doesn't know it was me. (*Round to front of desk*)

JO: You mean to say that your wife's family don't know that you're Paul Slickey?

JACK: You know what her father and the Great Man feel about each other. She'd cut my allowance if it came out.

JO: Your allowance? (*To* JACK)

JACK: You know me, kid. I have to live big! (*Embraces her.*)

13

JO: But, darling, they offered you dramatic criticism on the Globe. Why didn't you take that?

JACK: I take the theatre too seriously to be a dramatic critic. Another thing—my old man was in the business, and I know too much about it. It would show in no time, and I'd be out of a job again. Besides, you know I write plays myself.

JO: Do you know a critic who doesn't?

JACK: That's what I mean. Too much concentrated competition. Someday, people will find out what I'm really worth.

(*Quickly*) Why I was just a kid when I started. A kid out of the army when I won His Lordship's journalism scholarship. I was tough, I'd read books —I wanted to sleep with women! (*Kisses* JO *then returns to* C.) I had chips on my shoulder, holes in my socks, and a hard-hitting novel in my heart. I was a poor young reporter, and as I stood around sloshing back other people's champagne and eating their cold turkey and strawberries, I couldn't forget the shabby raincoat I'd left at the door!

(DANCERS *start to gather round. A* GIRL *walks provocatively past* JACK *and is glared at by* JO.)

Look at me now! Am I different? Have I changed? Am I just as talented as when I started out?

I'm just a guy called Paul Slickey, (*To downstage*)
And the job that I do's pretty tricky,
I'm twenty-eight years old
And practically everybody, anybody, anything
You can think of leaves me
Quite, completely
Newspaper neatly
Quite, quite cold.
Don't think you can fool a guy like me
The best things in life are never free!
Guys like us who are on the inside,
Cannot be taken for a ride.
We have professional ways and means

14

Of getting in behind the scenes,
To put the screws on stars in jeans.
We don't need hidden television screens.
Don't think you can fool a guy like me. (*To* L.)
There's nothing that's not like A.B.C.
(*To* R.) Guys like us who are on the spot,
Can be relied to know what's not,
Nothing's so big we can't shrink it—
We'll blot your lot and printers'-ink it,
Whatever slop you want we'll see you drink it,
(*To* L.)
We can't build your boat, but we'll make damn
    sure you sink it!

A shoddy little talent and a sawn-off imagination
Will never be allowed to go to waste,
While *we* have got our ear-holes to the heart-
    beat of the nation,
And our great big working finger on the moronic
    public taste.

So don't think you can fool a guy like me!
There's a woodworm in every family tree.
A princess or a premier can't ever come out
    rotten, (JO *curtseys then goes to desk.*)
But an actor or a writer must be somehow ill-
    begotten!

In my cashmere coat and my seat at the Caprice,
The newest public wonder waits my merciful
    release.
ALL: He'll build them up in Edinburgh and Nice,
    Until he tells the public they must cease!
JACK: I'll deride, I'll be snide, have no heart, I'll be smart.
ALL: For this is the age of the common man!
    (*Enter the* COMMON MAN.)
ALL: He'll be always on the band waggon, never in the
    cart

15

No one hates the simple little bastard like a
newspaper can.

JACK: Who are you?

C. MAN: I'm the common man.

JACK: Whose age is this?

C. MAN: Mine.

JACK: Who looks after your interests, protects your
freedom, upholds your glorious traditions and
institutions?

C. MAN: You do.

JACK: Who investigates vice, denounces prominent
homosexuals and Labour M.P.s who try to be
Socialists, disturbs you about the divorce rate and
the decline of your Christian heritage?

CHORUS: (*As each speaks his line, he comes downstage and
stays there*). Come off it you intellectuals!
British common-sense will always prevail!
What on earth are they angry about!
We are the majority, we are the ones who matter!
Most people are jolly hopeful, thank goodness!
I believe in Britain!
Life is quite morbid enough as it is!
We are solid and so are you.

JACK: Remember our brave fighting ships.
(*Lights dim except for a spot on* TWO MEN *with
naval caps and binoculars standing on desks* R.)

FIRST MAN: 30 seconds to zero.

SECOND MAN: Well, Hawkesworth, this is it. (*Pause*)

FIRST MAN: Yes sir. (*Pause*) What are you thinking, sir?

SECOND MAN: Thinking, Hawkesworth, thinking. I was just
wondering if Celia had remembered to pay the
boy's school fees in advance. Had a letter today.
He's made the first fifteen.

FIRST MAN: Oh, really, sir? You must be pretty proud of him.

SECOND MAN: (*thoughtfully*). Yes—I suppose I am. Decent kid.
Funny the things you think about at a time like
this.

FIRST MAN: Who do you fancy for the Cup Final, sir?

16

SECOND MAN: I've always been a Chelsea supporter myself.

FIRST MAN: I'd rather fancied Arsenal.

SECOND MAN: (*thoughtfully*). Arsenal. Good old Arsenal. Well, maybe you're right, Hawkesworth.

FIRST MAN: Five, four, three, two, one, zero.

SECOND MAN: Number one and two! Fire!

(*There is the sound of a terrific explosion.*)

C. MAN: That's what I call entertainment.

JACK: And he's right, in his funny little heart he's right!

(JOURNALISTS *quietly exit.* JACK *and* JO *kiss in the centre.*)

TELEPHONIST: Daily Racket. . . . Who? . . . Oh, just a moment.

(*Phone rings in the Slickey office.* JO *answers it.*)

JO: Slickey office. Oh yes, sir, just a moment. It's the great man for you.

(JACK *takes the receiver and sits on the desk.* JO *joins him and they kiss throughout the conversation.*)

VOICE: Oakham! Where have you been? Are you still working for me? I hear that Mortlake is ill again. He's only got a couple of days to make it. Get down there and see what's going on. It wouldn't surprise me if that old fraud were dead already and they were keeping it quiet! They've opened that place to the public at week-ends haven't they? But I hear you've got connections with that idiot family—is that right? Well, get down there and come back with something good!

(JO *replaces the receiver, and they break away.*)

JO: What did he mean—he might be dead already?

JACK: Old man Mortlake gave away his entire estate five years ago to the family to avoid death duties. Well almost five years—five years all but about forty-eight hours. If he doesn't last out the week-end the Income Tax Man will move in and whip the lot like a fully recovered German.

(JO *lies on* JACK'S *lap.*)

JO: It sounds like vintage Slickey. Go to it, boy!

JACK: Why can't someone else do it? Where's Joy?
JO: Paris.
JACK: Well, Sam then.
JO: You're a newspaperman, aren't you?
JACK: Well, Deirdre will be there. That's something I
suppose. (*Kisses* JO.)

  I'm just a guy called Paul Slickey,
(JO *sits up*.)
  And the job that I do's pretty tricky.
(JACK *stands on floor.* JO *fetches flower from desk,
hat and coat from stand and goes to* JACK.)
  I'm twenty-eight years old,
  And practically everybody, anybody, anything
(JACK *to* C.)
  You can think of leaves me
  Quite completely
  Newspaper neatly
(JO *puts the coat on* JACK'S *shoulders*.)
  Quite, quite cold. (JACK *puts coat on*.)
  So don't think you can fool a guy like me.
(JO *puts carnation in his buttonhole*.)
  There's woodworm in every family tree.
(JO *presents* JACK *with his hat, and then goes off
down* L.)
  A princess or a premier can't ever come out
   rotten,
  But an actor or a writer must be somehow
   ill-begotten.
  In my cashmere coat and my seat at the Caprice.
(*The keyhole cloth drops in behind* JACK *and the*
COMMON MAN.)
  The newest public wonder waits my merciful
   release.
  I'll build them up in Edinburgh and Nice,
  Until I tell the public they must cease.
  I'll deride, I'll be snide,
  Have no heart, I'll be smart,
  For this is the age of the common man.

I'll be always on the band waggon, never in the
    cart,
No one hates the simple little bastard like a
    newspaper can.

(JACK *exits down* R.)

C. MAN: (*produces a playbill from his pocket*). Where are
we? Hallelujah Productions present in association
with Gay Theatre Limited, Dame Penelope Smart
and Sir Wilfred Childs in "This is Our World" by
Beaumont Edner. Time: The Present. An early
evening in April. Place: a bedroom in Mortlake
Hall.

(BLACKOUT)

(*End of Scene One*)

(MUSIC)

ACT I

Scene Two

Mortlake Hall. The Marsden Room.
JACK *is sitting on a large bed. Beside him is* DEIRDRE RAWLEY. *She is wearing riding breeches and a slip.*

        (They embrace.)
        *(*DEIRDRE *stares up at him with soft eyes.)*

DEIRDRE: My darling—*(indicates clean sheets)*—I brought these—*(kisses him)*—to put on the bed. The visitors will be here very soon, gaping all over the place with their horrible guide books. It'll look very odd if they go into the Marsden Room and find the bed —well, unmade.

JACK: Isn't Cromwell supposed to have slept in it?

DEIRDRE: Yes, darling, but not last night. Have you got Michael's pyjamas there?

JACK: Here.

DEIRDRE: *(clasping them to her).* Oh, isn't this sordid!

JACK: Yes, it is rather.

DEIRDRE: I'm sorry you find it sordid.

JACK: Um?

DEIRDRE: Nothing. I just hoped you'd say it wasn't sordid because we really love each other.

JACK: Well, that's perfectly true I suppose——

DEIRDRE: No, you're quite right. It is sordid.

JACK: *(out of his depth).* Um!

DEIRDRE: Whether we love each other or not.
        *(*JACK *tries to think of something to say.)*

JACK: You didn't wake up Michael when you left?

DEIRDRE: Good lord no. Nothing wakes Michael. He just lies in bed all night, mumbling his beastly political speeches in his sleep. Oh, it's awful, I can't tell you!

JACK: Poor darling.

DEIRDRE: Do you know what he actually said to me the other night? He suddenly grabbed my shoulder in the middle of the night, and said, "away with party labels and let us pull together".

Oh, darling what are we going to do?

JACK: (*looking at sheets*). Make the bed I suppose. We've lain on our bed—and now we must make it.

DEIRDRE: Oh, Jack for heaven's sake——!

JACK: Sorry, darling.

DEIRDRE: It's just that these last few weeks have been so horrid what with having to be polite and casual with Lesley when she was here. I think she suspects.

JACK: I don't believe it.

DEIRDRE: What do you know about her! You're married to her.

JACK: I've known her like a rabbit knows an eagle.

DEIRDRE: (*stands*). I think you're a little hard on her, darling. After all, she may be your wife, but she's my sister. I daresay she's been a little upset about daddy. Just like we all have.

JACK: He's all right now, isn't he?

DEIRDRE: The doctor says the crisis has passed, but one still can't be quite sure when he'll collapse again. Why, the slightest thing might——

JACK: I didn't realize you were all so fond of him.

DEIRDRE: Of course we're fond of him—and Mummy's been so terribly brave.

JACK: Yes, she's always been a brave soul.

DEIRDRE: She has. I remember how she was when they gave away India. But she's been even more wonderful this time. Why, sometimes she seems so serene.

I've wondered if she's been aware of what is going on around her.

JACK: Kiss me.

(*They kiss on the bed.*)

DEIRDRE: Oh, my love, I am so afraid of it running out.

JACK: What?

DEIRDRE: Sex.

21

JACK: Running out? Like the coal mines, you mean.

DEIRDRE: No. I am afraid of it running out between us, you and me. I mean, suppose there really isn't anything else and it—runs out. What will happen? What will there be left for us?

JACK: We'll be in the desert and alone,
When we find our love has become overblown,
When the candle's lost its heat,
There'll be no market left for meat
We'll be in the desert and alone.

We'll be in the desert and alone,
We'll slip out of the cage and the bird will have flown,
When the springs on the bed start to rust,
There'll be nowhere to look for a crust,
We'll be in the desert and alone.

(*Kneels up.*)

The day is coming when mass diversions of the flesh will be launched like new washing powders by gigantic commercial empires in fierce competition with each other.

They'll take the "I" and the "Must" from our personal
Lust for a voice at a microphone.

DEIRDRE: Personally, I always use "slashit"! It doesn't merely satisfy, it actually kills desire.

The scientists and bishops are out to make us lump it
They'll make it much too hot for us to tackle any muffin.

BOTH: We'll be in the desert and alone,
Our song will be sung when our loins cease to groan,
Double crossing husbands with guilt-stricken stabs,
Will stop fishing for trouble and making any grabs.

22

Let passion go out of fashion!
Let the groin give a last great groan.
Let the lamb lie down with the lion
This fulfils our grand design.
We'll be in the desert,
We'll be in the desert,
We'll be in the desert and alone.
(*They kiss.*)

(BLACKOUT)

(*End of Scene Two*)

ACT I

Scene Three

The sitting-room.

DEIRDRE *is sitting on the sofa.* LADY MORTLAKE *enters through the french windows carrying an enormous bunch of flowers. She does very little else. She is in the long tradition of magnificently gracious ninnies so familiar to English play-goers. She is almost sixty and very, very handsome. She has passed through the recent "valley of the shadow" as if it were Trafalgar Square on Armistice Night.*

LADY M.: Oh if only one didn't have to work for one's living! It's such a glorious day full of sunshine and flowers.

DEIRDRE: Hello, Mummy.

LADY M.: Hello, dear.

DEIRDRE: Mummy, why is it that whenever I see you, you seem to be coming in with an enormous armful of flowers?

LADY M.: Do I?

DEIRDRE: It's just that you look like one of those incomparable actresses who make incomparable entrances from the french windows, bring on half a florist's shop with them and then spend most of the play arranging them wittily and ignoring the plot.

LADY M.: I wonder if that's where I first got it from! I've never been very fond of flowers as you know. I think one learns so much from the theatre, don't you? One can watch people as they really are and behave. All doing those tiny little things that seem to be so inconsequential at first glance but which are really quite fundamental and *full* of significance.

DEIRDRE: Oh, Mummy, those bloody flowers! (*Desperately*) Now you're going to arrange them, aren't you?

24

LADY M.: (*blandly*). Why, Deirdre, is anything the matter?
What dark rings you have around your eyes!
Couldn't you sleep, dear? I mustn't let you hold me
up this morning. I've just remembered—Mrs.
Giltedge-Whyte is coming here with that daughter
of hers and she's sure to come early. That sort of
woman always does.

DEIRDRE: Who is Mrs. Giltedge-Whyte?

LADY M.: George! Where's George? Where's your uncle?
Have you put him away yet?

DEIRDRE: Honestly, Mummy, I've had other things to do.
Anyway I haven't seen him.

LADY M.: Well, we must find him. The visitors will be coming
in very shortly and you know how he scares people
away.
(TREWIN *enters. An embittered man.*)
Trewin, have you seen Mr. George?

TREWIN: Not since breakfast, my lady.

LADY M.: Well, we must all look for him at once. Come
along everybody!
(*Exit*)

TREWIN: I believe he went down to the apple loft, madam.
He said he was going to write a letter to *The Times*.

DEIRDRE: Well, you'd better go down there and make sure
that he's put away.
(*Enter* MICHAEL RAWLEY. *He is about thirty-five, a
quintessential parliamentarian.*)

MICHAEL: Ah, Trewin, have you seen *The Times*?

TREWIN: I believe Mr. George has it, sir.

DEIRDRE: He's probably made a paper hat out of it now.

MICHAEL: Well, see what you can do, Trewin.

TREWIN: Very good, sir.
(*Exit*)

DEIRDRE: Do you know sometimes I am convinced that
Trewin despises us.
Do you think he's a Communist?

MICHAEL: I happen to know for a fact that Trewin has the
highest possible respect and admiration for private

25

enterprise. Why, he was a Trade Union Official for years. Until he was sent to Coventry by his workmates.

DEIRDRE: Poor Trewin, I had no idea!

MICHAEL: (*encouraged*). He became an outcast. Even his children suffered at school.

DEIRDRE: Oh, no!

MICHAEL: Yes, the other children would call out after them in the streets.

DEIRDRE: Call out?

MICHAEL: Yes, you know the sort of thing.

DEIRDRE: No, what sort of thing. (*Passionately*.) Go on, I *want* to know!

MICHAEL: (*hesitating*). Oh—vermin, boss crawlers, Tories, layabouts—pretty foul stuff like that.

DEIRDRE: Children can be so cruel.

MICHAEL: Trewin is like this house, Deirdre—solid! This has been a proud bastion of liberty for four hundred years. Its bulwarks are as sound as ever and I think we may safely say that the Mortlakes themselves have rendered a not unsignal service to their country in that time.

DEIRDRE: (*seeing an onslaught coming*). Yes, all right, dear.

MICHAEL: Do you know that there has actually been a legal agitation to turn this place into the County Headquarters of the National Assistance Board?

DEIRDRE: Oh, to think that Daddy might have actually died this week and left us all on the rocks! I go quite cold every time I think of it. Just one more day to get through. That's all, and then we'll be safe.

MICHAEL: We have come a long way, my dear, but we are not yet out of the wood.

DEIRDRE: Oh, for some peace! I feel so very tired.

MICHAEL: You do look rather whacked.

DEIRDRE: What?

MICHAEL: Whacked. Perhaps you're not getting enough sleep.

DEIRDRE: (*on guard*). What makes you say that?

MICHAEL: I don't know really. After all, we always go to bed pretty early. Even more so just lately.

DEIRDRE: (*near to hysteria by now*). Oh, my God, Michael—
don't!

MICHAEL: (*laying his hand on her shoulder*). I know how it is
old girl. I really do. Stick it out at all costs, my
dear, and I promise you we will win through
somehow to the end.

DEIRDRE: Michael—can't you see I am crying?

MICHAEL: I know, my dear, you go ahead. Deirdre, just
because I have been silent during the past few
weeks it does not mean that I have been unaffected
by what has been going on.

DEIRDRE: By what has been going on? You mean—you
know what has been going on?

MICHAEL: Make no mistake. I am more than ready to take
up the cudgels to defend what is mine.

DEIRDRE: Well I—I never thought you were so capable of
feeling so strongly about—that.

MICHAEL: I can't think why, Deirdre. After all this time, you
ought to know how strong my feelings are.

DEIRDRE: I'm quite taken aback, Michael. I am, really. You
must admit you've never said very much to me
about it—not even on our honeymoon.

MICHAEL: Nonsense. I distinctly remember discussing it
practically every night. Why, I spoke of it only the
other evening to the Chamber of Commerce.

DEIRDRE: The Chamber of Commerce! How could you?

MICHAEL: They were most enthusiastic I can assure you. I
tell you this, Deirdre: if by chance this situation
should call for desperate measures I shall not
hesitate to use them. A man still has some rights
left. I am prepared to go beyond the law if
necessary—to the House of Lords. Thank goodness
there are some representatives of the people left
who have their genuine interests at heart!

DEIRDRE: Michael—before I have hysterics! *What* are you
talking about?

MICHAEL: Why, the estate, of course. That's what we are

27

discussing, isn't it?

(*Enter* TREWIN *carrying "The Times" shaped into a hat which he hands to* MICHAEL.)

TREWIN: *The Times*, sir.

MICHAEL: Thank you, Trewin.

TREWIN: I've placed your bicycle in the drive, sir. I've looked all over the house for Mr. George, sir, but I can't find him anywhere.

MICHAEL: Good heavens, you don't think he's taking the money at the gates, do you? You'd better get down there at once.

(*Enter* LADY MORTLAKE.)

LADY M.: Ah, Trewin. I wish you would get someone to put that back door on. It's the first thing you notice when you come out of the North Gallery. It looks most unfortunate, especially as someone seems to have stored coal in the bathtub. People are only too anxious to jump to the wrong conclusion.

(*Exit* TREWIN.)

DEIRDRE: But surely no one could believe that—oh, how could they!

MICHAEL: No, Mother's quite right. Let us say at least that it is not an unjustifiable assumption.

DEIRDRE: Oh, my God! Michael do you ever *listen* to what you're saying?

MICHAEL: Most certainly, my dear. No one pays more scrupulous attention to the choice of words than I. The English language and its proper usage is a matter for our constant concern and vigilance. Oh, yes. It is a consideration which we should all do well to bear in mind.

> It's a consideration we'd do well to bear in mind
> You can play about with language in order to be kind
> The reason that we've always come through flourishing
> Is that English common sense is so astonishingly

28

nourishing
Other nations less endowed
Go along with all the crowd
Using logic and statistics
When all they need is parliamentary linguistics.

It's a consideration we'd do well to bear in mind
Gladstone must have said it on the day that he
   resigned
You only have to say in a lordly Oxford way
   without thought or any gumption
That "it's not an unjustifiable assumption"
Don't leave them any clues
While exploring avenues
And leaving stones unturned
If your words mean nothing, then your fingers
   won't get burned.

It's a consideration we'd do well to bear in mind
We can safely say in a not unpompous way,
   blind
Them with words! When there are things you
   can't mention.
Say "The Government is giving this matter its
   most grave and urgent attention"
If they're concerned about the atom
Simply hurl some clichés at 'em
If a problem's in a pressing condition
Give them words by the ton and the year—give
   them a Royal Commission.

LADY M.: Ah, they were always so useful. Freddie sat on one
once for nearly five years.

DEIRDRE: What was that about?

LADY M.: Something to do with the care and treatment of
children, I think. I know he didn't care for it. You
know how much he hates children.

MICHAEL: A good word nowadays is hard to find

29

We have it on the highest authority
That the present grievous anomaly
Is unlikely to last
We'll be caught up by the past
Give me sound, top peoples' phrases
To sing this country's praises
I will tell you with authority
And sensible sonority
Angry words are being touted
Ordinary decency is being flouted
By an irresponsible and unrepresentative majority.

It's a consideration we would all do well to bear
    in mind
It is not unsensible to sound stupid to be kind
To politicians words mean different things
You have to cheat on the roundabouts and
    swindle on the swings
When you've dropped your bombs first
And the other side has got the worst
Then your words must be strict
You're not at war, you—wait!—are in a state of
    armed conflict.
It's a consideration we'd do well to bear in mind.

This—is a consideration we would all do well to
    bear in mind
It is not unsensible to sound stupid to be kind
To politicians words mean different things
You have to cheat on the roundabouts and
    swindle on the swings
When you've dropped your bombs first
And the other side has got the worst
Then your words must be strict
You're not at war, you—wait!—are in a state of
    armed conflict.
It's a consideration we'd do well to bear in mind.

Well, the nation waits. Mustn't sit around. (*Kisses* DEIRDRE.) See you later, Deirdre. And do try to take things a little more calmly and clearly.

LADY M.: Take the laundry with you, will you.

MICHAEL: Of course. (*Picking up bag of laundry and "The Times".*) You see? A little intelligent discussion makes all the difference. 'Bye now.
(*Exit*)

DEIRDRE: Mummy—do you think Michael is a bore?

LADY M.: I can't really say. I've never listened to him very much. (*Perusing her correspondence*) If only we could afford to employ a secretary, even a temporary one.

DEIRDRE: I must say you're very brave to tackle it all on your own, darling.

LADY M.: (*smiling gently*). Ah, little do they know. No forty-four hour week for me. Deirdre, you seem jumpy this morning. Are you all right?

DEIRDRE: Oh, please don't make a fuss, Mummy. You know I can't bear a fuss.

LADY M.: This has been a terrible time for all of us. It's bound to take its toll. Thank heaven poor Freddie is his old self again. He wouldn't even let me help him down the stairs. He said he'd ring for Trewin.

DEIRDRE : I wish he wouldn't take such risks.

LADY M. : I think we can safely say that we have passed through our little valley of the shadow. I think Freddie had made up his mind that nothing was going to beat him.

DEIRDRE: How I wish I had his courage!

LADY M.: I know, dear, but very soon we shall be able to breathe like human beings again, which, after all, is what we really are, and then we can all go away for a nice long holiday. When I think of what this family has endured it makes me think back to that time just after the General Election in 1945.

31

DEIRDRE: There's no need to get morbid, Mummy. Besides all that's over and done with for good, thank heavens.

LADY M.: It isn't so easy for me to forget it, Deirdre.

DEIRDRE: Politics! God, I'm so bored with politics.

LADY M.: Well, after all, dear, you are married to a politician.

DEIRDRE: Mummy, I wish you wouldn't encourage Michael with his political career. I'd so much rather he did a job of work.

LADY M.: I suppose he could take a few directorships.

DEIRDRE: But darling, that wouldn't keep his *mind* occupied. Antonia's husband has got seventeen directorships and he hangs about the house all day making model boats. She says it's hell!

LADY M.: Naturally you're anxious for Michael to get somewhere soon. Don't worry, he will soon enough. He's already made an excellent start with the Young Conservatives. They've been most impressed by his initiative—Lady Bartlett was only telling me the other day. Do you know, they only had three tennis courts before he was elected Chairman and then those awful hard ones at that? And I do think you ought to remember that Michael has been denied many of the advantages that fall to more fortunate men.

DEIRDRE: I wouldn't call Eton, Oxford and the Guards exactly liabilities.

LADY M.: Those things are hardly advantages, Deirdre—any more than arms and legs are. Look at your father. I can't tell you how badly he started off. Somehow whenever a motion was being debated in the House he would invariably speak against it and vote for it. (*Enter* TREWIN.)

TREWIN: Mrs. Giltedge-Whyte, my lady.

(*Enter* MRS. GILTEDGE-WHYTE *and her daughter,* GILLIAN. MRS. GILTEDGE-WHYTE *is an attractive woman in her forties.* GILLIAN *is about eighteen and rather bored.*)

LADY M.: How sensible of you to come early!

(TREWIN *exits upstairs.*)

MRS. G.-W.: You really mustn't allow us to interrupt you, Lady Mortlake. Gillian and I can go and join the visitors looking round the house until lunch.

LADY M.: My correspondence—there's so much of it, I'm afraid.

MRS. G.-W.: Lady Bartlett tells me what sterling work you have done for her pet charities.

LADY M.: I don't believe you've met Mrs. Giltedge-Whyte, Deirdre.

MRS. G.-W.: How do you do?

DEIRDRE: How do you do?

MRS. G.-W.: My daughter, Gillian——

GILLIAN: Hi!

LADY M.: Mrs. Giltedge-Whyte wants me to arrange Gillian's coming-out for her.

MRS. G.-W.: I am a firm believer in professionals in all things.

DEIRDRE: I believe it.

LADY M.: Well, are you looking forward to your first Season, my dear?

GILLIAN: Good Lord, no! Everyone says it's terribly boring. Still, I suppose there's no alternative really, is there?

LADY M.: I suppose it's not quite the thrill it used to be for a young girl.

MRS. G.-W.: Ah! Before the war! Things will never be like that again, I'm afraid.

LADY M.: Some of us are doing our best.

GILLIAN: Do we have to pay half a crown to go round the rest of the house?

LADY M.: Only if you wish to, my dear. But you must wait until Freddie comes down. I know he'll be glad to meet you.

MRS. G.-W.: I've been such a devoted admirer of your husband for many years. (*Sits*) He has so many admirable qualities. He is a shining example to young people

C

33

like Gillian here. As for these people with their envy and class hatred, hanging is too good for them. How drab and uniform they wish to make life nowadays! And now they are trying to do the same thing with death. (*Rises and crosses to piano.*) These silly people who want to do away with capital punishment are a case in point. For myself, I'm all for doing away with the rope but after all human life is sacred and we must not allow people like murderers to escape just retribution. Besides, I hope I'm a Christian.

You may smile, my dear
But wait until you hear
Exactly what I feel
This thing inside that's a part
Of my deepest, dearest heart.
(*She moves to* C.)

Bring back the axe
Listen to the facts
The condemned man has died
What could be more dignified
Than his head on a plate
In a deterrent state
For a life to be ended
In a manner so splendid
Oh, why don't they bring back the axe.
(*Breaks* L. *to desk.*)
Bring back the axe
Listen to the facts
Hanging's so sordid and mean
The axe is so bright and so clean
Executions become so much duller
Oh, why don't they bring back some colour
The Welfare State is so drab
So give me his head on a slab
Oh, why don't they bring back the axe.

(*Breaks upstage to* C.)

    Bring back the axe
    Listen to the facts
    I long for the roll of the drums
    As on to the scaffold he comes
    Some gentle-eyed muscular artisan
    Oh what a beautiful hunk of man
    Sex-maniacs and perverts would dread
    The British tradition of losing your head.

(*Comes back to piano.*)

    Bring back the axe
    Forget psychological quacks
    For some brute who ill-treats a dog
    Or a horsey, or pussy would flog
    I'd send a warm invitation
    To his de-capitation
    We mustn't get soft but tough
    Hanging is simply not good enough
    So why don't they bring back the axe.

(*She flops her head and holds her arms at shoulder level. Then she crosses to the sofa and sits* R.)

The old ideals of duty and responsibility were so admirable, don't you think, Lady Mortlake?

LADY M.: Freddie's life has been a monument to them both. In fact, in recent years I believe that the purely spiritual values have become the only ones he prizes—or even recognizes.

(LORD MORTLAKE, *a bulky, shaky figure, obviously not very strong, and leaning heavily on* TREWIN, *starts to descend the stairs.*)

Ah, here comes Freddie now.

(LADY MORTLAKE *goes to stairs, and* MRS. GILTEDGE-WHYTE *to upstage of the sofa.*)

Do be careful, Freddie. Hold on to him tightly, Trewin.

TREWIN: (*panting*). Yes, my lady.

(LORD MORTLAKE *sees* MRS. GILTEDGE-WHYTE *for the first time. He looks as if he has been shot.*)

35

LORD M.: Good God, Ethel!

> (LORD MORTLAKE *begins to topple.* TREWIN *staggers under the overbearing strain, and* LORD MORTLAKE *falls heavily on the stairs.*)

(BLACKOUT)

(*End of Scene Three*)

ACT I

SCENE FOUR

In front of Mortlake Hall Gauze.
Enter Guide with tourists, journalists, etc.

GUIDE: Hey, Bob, did you get any good pictures?

PHOTOGRAPHER: Sure.

SCHOOLGIRL: I'll be glad to get out of this lot.

GUIDE: Say, you really do look like a tourist.

FIRST GIRL: Let's get back to the office.

SECOND GIRL: Glad I don't live here.

GUIDE: If you are going to live in a place like that, you've got to think big.

THIRD GIRL: They say this place was built by the third Earl of Mortlake.

GUIDE: That's how you've got to be if you are going to be a success, that is.

WENDOVER: Who was the first Earl of Mortlake?

GUIDE: The first Earl of Mortlake's name was Cedric. (*He throws his hat off downstage* R.)

CHORUS: Cedric?

GUIDE: (*coming* C. *Downstage.*)

> Now Cedric's daddy was a chappie
> Who couldn't make a damsel happy,
> He'd hardly got his bride
> Safely tucked in by his side
> When he quickly thought it wiser
> To re-adjust his visor.
> Leaping from his bridal bed,
> He preferred the friendship of his squire instead.
> And leaving Cedric's virgin mum

37

Set out for Jerusalem (*Moves* R.)
Saying, "No man wants some soppy maid
When he can have himself a gay Crusade!"
(*The men imitate a horse rider.*)
The years went by and Cedric's mum
One night, feeling very glum,
And wearing just her wedding ring
(*The "Queen" fingers a ring on her finger.*)
Sought the favours of the king.
So little Cedric, by-and-by
Became a gleam in the old king's eye.
While his should-be-dad fought heathen
    Turks,
His mum received the Royal works.
(*The "King" and "Queen" go into a clinch
downstage* R., *covered from the front by girls.*)
Soon one medieval morn
Little Cedric he was born,
(*"Cedric" appears downstage* R.)
And as his dad was still away,
(*"Cedric" kneels.*)
The king was prevailed upon to say:
"For his daddy's honour's sake,
(*"King" knights "Cedric".*)
I pronounce this bastard first Earl of
    Mortlake.
He's an illegitimate little mess,
(*"Cedric" cries.*)
But he's going to be a great success."
(*The Mortlake Gauze flies away and the office
is seen, with* JACK *sitting at his desk and* JO *on
it.*)
If you don't want to be an unidentified mess
You must make yourself Someone and be a
    success.
You've got to understand the mechanics of
    success
If you've meaning to express you must spell

it like success.

    If you're going to impress you must pander
        to the Press,

    They'll want you to assess how much money
        you possess,

    (GUIDE *crosses* R. *to* "*Actress*".)

      Don't feel distress if they malign your
        mistress,

      If they go to her address to photograph her
        in undress,

      You can forget her caress if you get your
        just redress,

      Fame's the best procuress, that's the Pattern
        of success,

      You've got to understand the mechanics of
        success.

JOURNALIST: Mr. Wendover Williams sat back in his antique
    Charles the Tenth chair and remembered his
    humble beginnings in a Nottingham rubber
    goods factory.

    (WENDOVER *crosses his legs*.)

    As he crossed his legs in his beautiful Savile
    Row suit, I said to him: now that you are
    Somebody don't you feel you are in danger of
    becoming a corrupt Nobody? Flicking the ash
    of his personally monogrammed cigarette from
    his twenty-five carat gold cigarette holder, he
    replied.

WENDOVER: Well, I must admit I began to wonder that
    myself the other day when I bought my first
    five hundred stocks in British Steel.

JOURNALIST: Already you feel that your values are changing?

WENDOVER: That's a weird question!

JOURNALIST: He stammered guiltily and called languidly for
    another bottle of champagne.

WENDOVER: Hey, Mabel! Another light ale, please.

    (MABEL *brings him a glass of ale*.)

JOURNALIST: And I put another question to the man who

said recently that the Tories were burglars, berks and bloodlusters.

WENDOVER: Have a Woodbine? (*Brings out a packet.*)

JOURNALIST: Do you find, now that you have five hundred shares in British Steel, that you are worried about Nationalization?

WENDOVER: Should I worry?

JOURNALIST: What about your Socialist views now?

WENDOVER: If the Labour Party Nationalizes Steel, I'll be so overcompensated I'll probably be better off than ever. (WENDOVER *laughs, then drinks.*)

JOURNALIST: Mr. Williams scowled savagely and said that as long as he got his money he didn't give a damn.

WENDOVER: Like a packet of crisps to go with that? (MABEL *brings the crisps, and he tears the packet open and eats with relish.*)

JOURNALIST: What, I said, as he tucked into his salmon at eighteen shillings a pound, does your wife say about your success?

WENDOVER: Well, I can't say we've ever discussed it much.

JOURNALIST: He said that he and his wife had not been on speaking terms for some time.

WENDOVER: Well, thanks for the sandwich. I must go home and get on with some work. 'Bye. Taxi! (*Takes his chair back upstage* R.)

JOURNALIST: And so, stepping into his gleaming Mercedes sports car, he left me—off to another gay round of parties. There, I thought, goes a success.

> You've got to understand the mechanics of success,

(*He goes to* ACTRESS *on* R.)

> A mediocre young actress need not rely on her mattress,
> But if from acting she'll digress and stick to publicity finesse
> She can be as wet as watercress and still be

40

a success. (*To* C.)
And you will say to the ultimate journalist,
as he leans unsteadily against the bar of deceit,
as he asks the questions that prevent real
questions being asked, you will look up into
his face and say: (*Kneels downstage* C.)
　　Because of you, I am,
　　Before, I never was, but now I exist,
　　You drink, therefore I am.
(*He clasps* JO.)
　　Every editor and every editress must be your
　　　dictator and dictatress
　　Match your poor seductiveness against this
　　　goddam bitch success.

GUIDE: You may not have prowess but who the
　　　hell's to guess,
　　As long as somehow you progress, we'll give
　　　you happiness.
　　You've got to understand, you've got to
　　　understand,
　　You've got to understand the mechanics of
　　　success.
(*Dancers and* GUIDE *go off downstage* L *and
downstage* R.)

JO: Is that all? (*Rises*)
JACK: Isn't it enough?
JO: The Honourable Penelope Cumming—well, I
suppose she's always worth a few inches.
(*Reading*) "Lady Poon-Tang, who is expecting
her third baby early this summer. . . . And a
beautiful new face this season, Miss Poppy
Tupper." What about Deirdre Rawley?
JACK: How can I do that?
JO: If you don't, someone else will. And what about
his lordship—old man Mortlake?
JACK: But I'm a guest——
JO: Does that usually stop you?
JACK: Not only that—I'm a relative.

41

JO: So?

JACK: (*rises*). So there are such things as trust, loyalty, honest intentions.

JO: And?

JACK: There are excesses.

JO: There are?

JACK: There are times when you must——

JO: What?

JACK: Not exploit other people's misery. (*Sits on desk.*)

JO: I didn't notice you helping the woman in that factory blaze last month. We couldn't even publish the pictures you took. (*Moves downstage of desk.*)

JACK: It was a great story, wasn't it?

JO: Inhuman interest.

JACK: Endeavour isn't my line of country. You know as well as I do—it's just a gimmick.

JO: Then what about the Deidre Rawley story?

JACK: You wouldn't do that to me? (*Sits on desk and cuddles up to* JO.)

JO: (*putting arms round him*). What will you do for me?

JACK: Dinner at the Caprice?

JO: That place!

JACK: The Milroy?

JO: *You* know how to keep me quiet.

JACK: I'm married. (*Sits up.*)

JO: So is Deirdre Rawley. (*Rises*)

JACK: Somewhere in all this chaos there must be some values I want to preserve.

JO: That's for the leader page: this united commonwealth family, our lifeline that must be preserved at the expense of British soldiers shot in the back three times a week, the treasure of family life, sexuality without sin, strengthening our ancient ties across the Atlantic, our supply of bombs and Coca-Cola to the troubled

42

areas of the world, simple words but true, the beauty of the ceremonial, the essential spirituality of the rite!

JACK: There must be a place for me somewhere in all this!

JO: (*sits and takes* JACK'S *head on her lap*). For both of us, darling. There's nothing in this world you can't get from me. Me and money. You do want that too, don't you? Don't you ever want to drink champagne you've paid for yourself? Don't you want to sit in the sun and write that play?

JACK: Are you kidding?

JO: Well—what about Lord Mortlake? What's the dope? Do you realize the old man's been ringing for you every ten minutes. He seems to feel that your painstaking literary style may not be finding its real outlet with a newspaper like us.

JACK: (*sits up*). It's all right for him—playing about in the South of France with six telephones, a couple of film starlets and a cabinet minister.

JO: Don't worry, darling. (*Close to him*) Stay with me. You can go back to Mortlake in the morning.

JACK: (*pulls away so that* JO *falls on desk*). Why do people use their bodies as points of escape and not as objects of love?

JO: There! You'll write that hit one day. I know it. And then they'll be writing about you. (*Sits on edge of desk*.)

JACK: Imagine it—me in Paul Slickey's column. With Lady Penelope Cumming, and another beautiful new face this season, Miss Poppy Tupper. Am I as trivial as this? (*Moves to* R. *of desk*.)

JO: Great men are easily discredited.

ACK: Could I be great? (*Sits on desk*.)

JO: (*softly*). I'll tell you later. I'm going to change.

43

Don't go away.
(*Exits* R.)

JACK: You stand there to remind me
        Wherever I look
        You're always there behind me.
        The Image with a smile so sweet
        Of the thing I can't defeat.
        Tell me later
        Don't tell me now.
        If I avoid those quiet eyes
        I might learn how to be wise
        So tell me later
        Don't tell me now.

        Our love has lost its shape.
        It's an instrument
        You run up to escape
        The we of me
        Is the longing to be free
        Tell me later
        Don't tell me now
        Just wrap your arms around
        My brain won't make a sound
        But tell me later
        Don't tell me now.

(*He moves downstage* R.; *the Keyhole cloth
comes in behind him and he goes to the* R. *pros.*)

        Why am I here?
        What am I doing?
        What am I thinking of?
        I've got nothing but trouble brewing!
        What am I living for?
        I'm living from mouth to mouth
        Going from your door to your door!

        This matter of living
        With its loving
        Its pretention of giving

Its cream cheeks, its deception
Its whispered imperception
Tell me later
Don't tell me now
The lies we long to mutter
As you love me in my gutter
Tell me later,
Tell me later,
Don't tell me now.
Don't tell me now.

(BLACKOUT)

(*End of Scene Four*)

ACT I

SCENE FIVE

Evening of the same day.
The stage is empty.
There is a sharp clanging, as the front doorbell rings. At the top window appears a stern little man of about sixty-five. He is dressed in eighteenth-century clothes and wears a rather rakish wig. He stops and listens intently. He chuckles, and comes downstairs. Hearing the sound of approaching voices from the hall, he hovers round the open door, and then, as they get nearer he goes off, through the panel in the wall upstage R. TREWIN *enters with* LESLEY OAKHAM. *She is tall, very beautiful and superbly dressed.* MICHAEL *follows them.*

LESLEY: I was in the middle of a board meeting when Mother rang me. . . . I couldn't get away sooner. How is he?
(She starts to take her coat off and puts her bag on the sofa. TREWIN *exits upstage* L.)

MICHAEL: Just about the same.

LESLEY: Who is with him now?

MICHAEL: Father Evilgreene.

LESLEY: Father Evilgreene?

MICHAEL: Good heavens, Lesley. You're looking pretty magnificent, if I may say so.

LESLEY: You may.

MICHAEL: May I—may I kiss you?
(She inclines her head towards him and he kisses her gingerly.)

LESLEY: Oh, do be careful, Michael!
(She takes out a handmirror, peers at her face crossly.)

MICHAEL: So sorry, my dear. It just seems so long since I

46

saw you.

LESLEY: Does it? It's only five days. Pour me a drink.
Who is this Father Evilgreene?

MICHAEL: (*pours drinks at the piano*). Your father asked for
him soon after he collapsed. Don't care much for
the fellow myself. Looks altogether too cheerful
for my taste. He's been up there since tea-time.
Ate a whole trayful of fish-paste sandwiches and
then sent down for some more. Astonishing
appetite. Nothing of him either.

LESLEY: How long is there to go now?

MICHAEL: (*crosses to* LESLEY *with the drinks*). Just a matter
of hours, my dear. If we lose this race against
time, I feel that we shall not only be betraying
ourselves but the country itself and all it stands
for.

LESLEY: I can't understand why you haven't got into
Parliament yet, Michael. I certainly thought you
would get into East Molesworth that last time.
Wasn't it supposed to be a stronghold?

MICHAEL: It was. Couldn't understand it. I based almost my
entire campaign on giving the H-bomb to the
Germans. Half the town was destroyed in air
raids during the war, so I thought they would have
a particular interest in foreign policy. I'm afraid
the electorate can be very irresponsible at times.
You know, Lesley, I feel very strongly about all
this, I can tell you. (*Sits on piano stool.*)

LESLEY: Who doesn't! I'm tired of all these miserable little
people who want to take everything away from us.
Something should be done about it. (*Crosses to*
MICHAEL.)

    I have a secret plan and because I love you
    I should like to tell you all about it.
(*She pulls* MICHAEL'S *arm back.*)
    This is what's happened to British aggression
    It's all concentrated on this one obsession.
(*She strangles* MICHAEL.)

47

We want to screw, screw, screw the Income Tax
　　Man
(*She pulls him to* c. *and throws him on the floor.*)
　　Screw him down as hard as ever we can
　　Take him, break him, scrape him, rape him
(*She steps downstage over him.*)
　　We're going to screw, screw, screw the Income
　　　　Tax Man.

　　How can you describe him
　　He's weak and small
　　He is flabby and he's tall
　　He's hairy all over and his face is red
　　Just imagine him in bed, aa-aah.
(MICHAEL *rises and comes downstage.*)

MICHAEL:　He's the canker in your ear.
LESLEY:　How can you make him disappear?
MICHAEL:　He's sadistic, atavistic
　　　　He's a cad, ask your dad.
LESLEY:　He's contrary, he's a swishy,
　　　　He's a disappointed lover.
MICHAEL:　He's a man without a mother
　　　　He's a schmo, he's a schmock.
LESLEY:　His home life is disturbing
　　　　He's irrevocably suburban.
(*They face* R.)
BOTH:　And think of him at school
　　　　When he never played the fool.
LESLEY:　When he played with little girls.
MICHAEL:　I hope they pulled his little curls.
LESLEY:　I'll bet he never made a noise.
MICHAEL:　I'm sure he played with horrid toys.
LESLEY:　And what about his wife,
　　　　What about that poor bitch's life?
BOTH:　We want to screw, screw, screw the Income Tax
　　　　Man.
　　　　Screw him down as hard as ever we can
　　　　Take him, break him, scrape him, rape him,

48

We're going to screw, screw, screw the Income
      Tax Man.

LESLEY: (*to downstage* R.) He is mintsy and he's chintzy.

MICHAEL: (*to downstage* L.) He is prissy, he's a cissy.

LESLEY: He is there, everywhere
        Like a louse in your hair.

MICHAEL: He is on your head,
        In your bed,
        In your ear, in your beer.

LESLEY: While you're being inventive
        He'll ruin your incentive.

MICHAEL: He's longing to hear the sound
        Of nineteen and six in the pound,
        He's got bad breath.

LESLEY: He's the new Black Death.

(*During the next few lines they point at the
audience from* L. *to* R.)

BOTH: He is watching, watching, watching every one
        of you,
        The man we all want to screw,
        Commissioner of Inland Revenue.

        We want to screw, screw, screw the Income Tax
        Man,
(*To* C.)
        Screw him down as hard as ever we can,
(*They face together.*)
        Break his back, on the rack, sew him up in a
        sack,
        Weight him down with irons,
        Throw him to the lions
        Before we end our Island story
        Let's have our last bit of hope and glory
(LESLEY *curtseys.*)
        On the day, on the wonderful day,
        That we screw, screw, screw the Income Tax
        Man!
(*They run to sofa, collapse on to it and kiss. Then*

break apart. MICHAEL *goes and sits again on the piano stool.*)

MICHAEL: Oh, I wish I knew what was going to happen to us all, Lesley. Seeing Jack here today doesn't make me feel any better. Between ourselves, I can't help feeling that he's on to us. Do you think it's possible?

LESLEY: That he knows about us? Quite. (*Rises and sits in Gothic chair.*) Jack has an odd feminine instinct about that sort of thing. He's extraordinarily passionate, you know. I think he must get it from his family. His mother is a charlady or something, I believe.

MICHAEL: Deirdre's rather the same.

LESLEY: It would be so like Jack to tread all over her with his great romantic boots on.

MICHAEL: Good heavens! (*Rises*) You don't think that Jack and Deirdre——

LESLEY: All I know is that Jack has always suffered from excessive aspiration. There is a constant stain of endeavour underneath his emotional armpits. It throws off quite an unpleasant smell of sour ideals.

MICHAEL: Deirdre and Jack! I can't believe it. Why, I remember the very first day I met her. (*Crosses to sofa.*)

LESLEY: At the gymkhana, wasn't it?

MICHAEL: Yes, grand little horsewoman, Deirdre. And then at the Primrose League Conference later. Why, she seemed utterly sound through and through.

LESLEY: I think that's why I admire you, Michael. Even if your judgments aren't usually correct, you're so clear-sighted and level-headed.

MICHAEL: You don't think Deirdre would want a divorce, do you?

LESLEY: I've no idea. You said she was a romantic.

MICHAEL: But it's unthinkable.

LESLEY: Of course. I should never be able to talk to you

50

in the Royal Enclosure.

MICHAEL: Good heavens, I hadn't thought of that! Lesley, what a penetrating intellect you have.

LESLEY: Simply free of bias and self-deception that's all.

MICHAEL: (*goes to* LESLEY). My dear, if Deirdre did try to force me into a divorce, would you want to marry me?

LESLEY: I'm quite content with the present arrangement. Besides I don't really approve of divorce.

MICHAEL: I must say you'd be a magnificent asset to a man with a career like myself.

LESLEY: (*rises downstage*). Now you are talking exactly like Jack. He always wanted me to be an asset to him in his career. You must realize, Michael, it is no longer a woman's job to make a hero of her man, but to be a hero unto herself.

MICHAEL: (*aghast with admiration*). Ah, yes. Quite right, my dear, quite right. May I?
(*They embrace by the piano.*)
Good God, Lesley, you are a remarkable woman!
(*He kisses her again.*)

LESLEY: (*calmly*). You're steaming my glasses.

MICHAEL: Damn your glasses!

LESLEY: Michael, really!

MICHAEL: (*passionately*). Damn them, I say! Take them off!
(*She hesitates.*)
Take them off!

LESLEY: There are moments, Michael, when I wonder whether you are all man after all. (*She takes them off.*)

MICHAEL: By heaven, I wish I were! And you were all woman!

LESLEY: Impossible, I'm afraid.
(*They embrace again.*)
No, Michael, I couldn't marry you. Marriage is quite disgusting. For one thing it makes intimacy quite impossible. To say nothing of passion.

MICHAEL: Oh, my dear, you're so full of wit. (*Laughs*)

LESLEY: I beg your pardon?

MICHAEL: What's that old tag? Someone's carved it on the door in the North Gallery. Ah, "One would think from all this wit, that T. S. Eliot had written it."

LESLEY: (*coldly*). I think epigrams are so shoddy. Why are you staring, is my nose shiny or something?
(*She goes to her handbag, and powders her nose.*)

MICHAEL: Lesley—another thought has occurred to me. If a whisper of any scandal were to get to your father's ears, he'd move heaven and earth to change any financial arrangements he'd already made on our behalf. You realize that?

LESLEY: But surely if everything's legal, there's nothing that he can do about it at this stage?

MICHAEL: Legal be damned! He can soon get a lawyer to change that. My darling!
(*They embrace again, and a long shadow falls swiftly across the head of the stairs.*)

LESLEY: Sh!

MICHAEL: What is it?

LESLEY: There's someone on the stairs.
(*They both look up. The figure on the stairs is* FATHER EVILGREENE. *A tall spare man with a short stubble of hair and ravaged cheekbones. The smouldering fires behind his eyes seem to have charred black-edged pits in his face. Being tall, he can look all around him without the necessity of ever having to look into anyone's face.* MICHAEL *and* LESLEY *break apart.*)

MICHAEL: Father Evilgreene! You startled us.
(FATHER EVILGREENE *shoots a long, quick glance round.*)

FATHER E.: I'm afraid *I* was lost in silent prayer. (*Descending.*) I'm so sorry.

MICHAEL: Oh, I daresay we are a little on edge, you know. It's understandable in the circumstances.

FATHER E.: Quite.

MICHAEL: Ah—this is Mrs. Oakham.

52

FATHER E.: Your wife's sister, isn't it? I remember you very well. (*He strokes her arm.*)

LESLEY: Do you? (*Breaks away and sits in the Gothic chair.*)

FATHER E.: Yes, very well indeed. I visited your father once before many years ago when he was going through a similar spiritual crisis. A very pretty little girl you were—yes, very pretty indeed. I believe you've made a highly successful career for yourself. What is it you do now?

LESLEY: Well, I dabble a little in show business—among other things I manage Terry Maroon.

FATHER E.: Terry Maroon? Ah yes, the—pop singer.

LESLEY: You've heard of him?

FATHER E.: Mrs. Oakham, even I have heard of Terry Maroon. He seems to be a very pleasant young man. Most sincere too, I imagine.

LESLEY: Oh, he's sincere all right.

MICHAEL: She's also the managing director of the Blossoming Treasure Brassière Company.

FATHER E.: How interesting. (*Takes two long steps to* LESLEY.)

LESLEY: Oh, it is. We have placed the female bosom higher and rounder than ever before.

FATHER E.: My own efforts seem humble indeed compared with yours.

LESLEY: Not at all, Father. The Blossoming Treasure Brassière functions in exactly the same way. It does its work not by pressure, but by brilliant design.

(FATHER EVILGREENE *backs up into* MICHAEL, *who is startled.*)

MICHAEL: How is Lord Mortlake, Father?

FATHER E.: He will find his peace soon—one way or another. He is fighting very hard. In the meantime, I wonder if I might have a little food? No, don't bother, I know my way. (*Starts to exit upstage* L.)

LESLEY: I hope you've locked the wine cellar.

(FATHER EVILGREENE *turns, grins hideously, and goes.*)

53

MICHAEL: Lesley, that remark is in pretty bad taste.

LESLEY: Oh!

MICHAEL: One must be careful at all times not to hurt other people's feelings whatever may be your own private opinion. Only an extremely vulgar mind pokes fun at such things.

LESLEY: Of course, you're perfectly right. (*Advances seductively on* MICHAEL.)

MICHAEL: I didn't mean to sound harsh, my dear.
(*They embrace.*)
Lesley I—do you think we could——

LESLEY: If you wish.

MICHAEL: Oh!

LESLEY: We can go up to the Marsden Room.

MICHAEL: Yes, let's. (*Grabs her impulsively.*) Lesley!

LESLEY: Well?

MICHAEL: Whatever happens we must not go back to physical controls, rationing or restrictions.

LESLEY: Bring my coat with you. (*She opens secret door— as she turns away* JACK *slips in through door, and into upstage* R. *arch.*)

LESLEY: Hurry up.
(*A photographer appears at the head of the stairs.*)

MICHAEL: Oh, my God!

LESLEY: (*pulling him after her*). Come on!
(*They exit through the secret door, which shuts behind them.*)

JACK: (*re-entering and picking up telephone*). Give me Fleet Street, 10,000.

(BLACKOUT)

(*End of Scene Five*)

ACT I

Scene Six

"The Daily Racket". JO *is standing by* JACK'S *desk*, JACK *by the hatstand. He looks troubled.*

JO: Hullo. (*He dosen't answer her. She kisses him.*)

JACK: Well?

JO: Nothing. Perhaps I really enjoy being simply a variation of your usual performance. What have you been doing?

JACK: Performing, I suppose.

JO: You're in today's bulletin, by the way.

JACK: Oh!

(JO *goes up to the bulletin board and takes the bulletin down.*)

JO: Yes, you and Charlie Fudge come in for practically the lot. (*Reading*) "Congratulations to Charles Fudge on today's lead story. This really got over the terrible drama of an Iron Curtain intellectual's constant agony of mind and ever-present physical danger—without, incidentally, letting it be known that most of this stuff was told in complete confidence to Fudge and that this man's existence is now more in danger than ever."

JACK: (*takes the bulletin from her*). "A touch of genius this, Charlie. Full marks for a piece of top-flight, political journalism told in real, human terms."

JO: Good old Fudge!

JACK: Well, he's got a nose for it all right.

JO: He should get round to smelling himself sometime. (*She takes the bulletin from* JACK *and reads. Reading.*) "Why nothing more on Mortlake?

55

   (*Moves to upstage of desk.*) Somebody will scoop
   us on this, if someone doesn't take it out and get
   stuck in!" What's the matter?

JACK: I'm just wondering why do I have to compete.

 JO: You've got to.

JACK: Couldn't I be something else? (*Sits on desk.*)

 JO: Why do you concern yourself with everybody else
   —let them do the worrying. (*Exits R.*)
   (*The lights fade out except for a spot on* JACK.
   JACK *moves downstage R.*)

JACK: Why am I here?
   What am I doing?
   What am I thinking of?
   I've got nothing but trouble brewing,
   What am I living for?
   I'm living from mouth to mouth
   Going from your door to your door.
   (*Music changes.*)
   There must be something I can do,
   Something to believe,
   Something better, something matters,
   There's someone to grieve,
   Somewhere better, somewhere finer,
   There must be something I can do!
   (*The lights come up.*)
   Ah, well! Who cares! Who cares!
   Who the devil cares!

CHORUS: They do! (*Point out front.*)

JACK: Who do?

CHORUS: They do! (*Point out front.*)

JACK: They?

CHORUS: Them! (*Point out front.*)

JACK: Them? Who's them?

CHORUS: The ones we're not!

JACK: Who's that?

CHORUS: Him!

   (*From their centre they push out the* COMMON MAN.
   He is reading "The Daily Racket".)

C. MAN: Pardon me! I'm not one of them, thank you very much. (*Exits downstage* L.)

JACK: Well, who is he?

(*All accuse the audience.*)

Them! It's them!
It's not us, it's not you
But it's them!

CHORUS: Them! Them! Them! Them!

JACK: This island of phlegm,
It's our staple apology,
Our apophthegm,
It's them! Them!

CHORUS: Sh! Sh! Sh!
Sh! Sh! Sh!
We must think it, we must say it,
In our pubs we'll never nay it,
Don't try to write it,
You're never going to fight it!

(*Dance*)

JACK: Them! Them! Them!
Sing a daily requiem,
They may be half unconscious
But it's not our problem
It's them! It's them! It's them!

CHORUS: Sh! Sh! Sh! Sh! . . .

(*They go off* L. *in line.*)

(JACK *is left alone in the centre of the stage, facing upstage, as the tabs fall.*)

(*End of Act I*)

ACT II

SCENE SEVEN

The offices of "The Daily Racket". SECRETARY *and* SEVERAL JOURNALISTS.
The sound of a linotype operator.

JO: (*on phone*). No—wait a minute. Jack—don't hang up yet. The old man's going crazy for something from Mortlake. And so am I, darling. What on earth are you doing down there? What. . . . Is she? Behaving like Lady Chatterley on Ice? Well, she's your wife. . . . Who's coming? Deirdre? Oh, all right then. But you'd better ring back with something soon. . . . (*Hangs up. To* LADY JOURNALIST.) Lady Chatterley on Ice? Perhaps I should go down there and see what's going on.

LADY JOURN.: Why don't we all go down? I know Deirdre awfully well. And, of course, I've known Lesley for years.

JO: Ladies, ladies, think of your editions!
Edna Francis-Evans:
Write of politicians' wives
Important in your readers' lives.

Cornelia Tuesday:
Some crackling observations
On the U.S. Air Force stations.

Belgravia Lumley:
What about this New Line?
Can't you say it's *not* divine?

And you—Ida Merrick:

When you write about the heart
Your wit is positively tart!

Ladies, ladies, think of your editions
Of a spanking line about boring social missions.

Edna Francis-Evans! Here!
Cornelia Tuesday! Here!
Belgravia Lumley! Here!
And you—Ida Merrick! Oh, here, I suppose.
Ladies, ladies, remember your best position.

JO *with* SIX SMART LADY JOURNALISTS:

Put it on ice
On ice! On ice!
If it's cool
It's sure to be nice
If it's dreary
Pretty weary
The whole thing looks better on ice!

Put it on ice!
On ice! On ice!
If you're clever
It's cheap at the price
If you want to skate
On your fate
Put yourself bang on the ice!

Put it on ice!
On ice! On ice!
If you're bright
You can cut you a slice
Don't give yourself trouble
Let the others bubble
Keep your nose clean on the ice!

(MEN JOURNALISTS *enter downstage* L.)
(*Ballet*)

ALL: Put it on ice!

59

On ice! On ice!
Being hot's
An unfashionable vice
If you let off steam
You're no maiden's dream.

JO: Why don't you get a licence for that
Thing and walk it round the park!

ALL: Put the whole thing back on the ice!
(*Passionate* MEN JOURNALISTS *dance with freezing*
LADY JOURNALISTS.)

LADIES: Please do not sneeze
We're in a deep freeze
Just take our tips
Those burning lips
Give us the pips.

JO *with* SIX SMART LADY JOURNALISTS *and* MEN JOURNALISTS

MEN: Get in those bunks
You icy chunks.

LADIES: Stand back you punks!

Put it on ice!
On ice! On ice!
With the women
Don't let's tell you twice
When you write your column
Be sparkling not solemn
Pack yourself
Wrap yourself
Stack yourself
Up to your freezing eyelashes in ice!
In ice!

JO'S VERSE:

Ladies, ladies, think of your
Editions!

Edna Francis-Evans;
Tell us what you think of men,
How to give them hell—and when!

60

Cornelia Tuesday;
Help us out of sexual muddle,
What's the newest way to kiss and
Cuddle?

Belgravia Lumley;
Write something about Modern Art,
Bitchy, brittle, awfully smart.
And you—Ida Merrick;
However things may worsen,
You'll always be a Fun Person.

Ladies, ladies, think of your
Editions!
Sink in your finger-nails, make
Your incisions!
(*Cha-cha-cha Dance.*)
(*Keyhole and blacks drop in during dance.*)
(*Keyhole and blacks away.*)

(*End of Scene Seven*)

ACT II

Scene Eight

Mortlake Hall.
MRS. GILTEDGE-WHYTE *at desk and* GILLIAN *in gothic Chair.*

MRS. G.-W.: If you're bored, Gillian, I'm sorry, but I'm afraid I really have no patience with you. I could have made all the arrangements for your coming-out with Lady Mortlake on my own quite easily.

GILLIAN: I just thought there might be a chance of meeting someone who could get me a job.

MRS. G.-W.: As an actress? Honestly, Gillian, if I had thought you wanted to be an actress I would never have sent you to the Academy of Dramatic Art.

GILLIAN: Well, it doesn't seem much fun sitting about here waiting for the old boy to kick it off.

MRS. G.-W.: Don't be unfeeling, Gillian. Besides, we don't know that Lord Mortlake is going to die at all. Oh, I think it's magnificent the way these old families are battling on. (*She rises.*) You see, Gillian, my dear, you can't destroy the really worthwhile things. Somehow they've a way of winning through in the end. No, I don't think the Mortlakes will let us down.

GILLIAN: I suppose it will be one in the eye for the Government if he does hang on.

MRS. G.-W.: And they deserve it. They deserve much more.

GILLIAN: You do sound a bit barbaric sometimes.

MRS. G.-W.: I'm afraid, like so many people, you're inclined to be sentimental about these things, Gillian. I've noticed it before. Ever since we had to eat your bunnies during the war.

62

GILLIAN: Oh, Mummy, don't!
(*Enter* GEORGE *still dressed in eighteenth-century costume through the secret panel.*)

MRS. G.-W.: Oh! Good evening.
(GEORGE *nods.*)
I don't think we've been introduced.
(GEORGE *takes out a snuff box and taps it.*)

GEORGE: (*offering box*) Snuff?

MRS. G.-W.: No, thank you, I never take it.

GEORGE: Just as well. I haven't got any.
(*Exit* GEORGE *up stairs*)

GILLIAN: Why do you suppose he dresses like that?

MRS. G.-W.: Surely it's symbolic!

GILLIAN: He's strictly from Cubesville. (*She rises to piano.*)
I wonder if they've got any records for that thing.
Why, there's a whole stack of Terry Maroon's here. How marvellous!
(*A bent figure staggers into view at the top of the stairs. It is* LORD MORTLAKE. *He leans heavily against the staircase and glares down.*)

MRS. G.-W.: Why, Lord Mortlake, what are you doing out of bed?

LORD M.: Are you still here?

MRS. G.-W.: Is there anything we can do for you?

LORD M.: No, damn it. Help me down these stairs.

MRS. G.-W.: But——

LORD M.: Oh, don't argue!

MRS. G.-W.: Well, you really must be careful. Lady Mortlake would be most upset if she were to see you.

LORD M.: I'll bet. The whole crew of 'em too. Just give me a hand down and shut up. And tell that girl to go.
(GILLIAN *moves upstage to* MRS. GILTEDGE-WHYTE.)

MRS. G.-W.: This is my daughter Gillian.

LORD M.: Oh, is it?

MRS. G.-W.: She's pretty, don't you think?

LORD M.: Too blasted pretty.

MRS. G.-W.: Gillian, you'd better go into the library. You can take your Mr. Maroon with you if you like.

63

GILLIAN: Oh, all right.
(*Exit upstage* L. *with records.*)

LORD M.: All right, all right. I'll sit here. (*Both sit on stair-case.*) Now, Ethel, what are you doing here? What do you want?

MRS. G.-W.: Why, I came to see you, Freddie. Aren't you pleased to see me after all these years?

LORD M.: Why can't you leave me to die in peace!

MRS. G.-W.: You needn't worry, Freddie. I have no intention of telling anyone about us.

LORD M.: Thank heaven for that! I need hardly say that it was a great shock seeing you here this morning. I have to be so extremely careful. So many people look up to me, Ethel. Not only my family, but people who matter—the Press, the leaders of Church and State. It hasn't been easy, believe me; but after all one must believe in something. Otherwise there's nothing left except the transient joys of personal pleasure. (*Eyeing her warily.*)

MRS. G.-W.: How proud you look in your pyjamas, Freddie! You never used to wear pyjamas. (*Puts her hand on his knee, and he hastily removes it.*)

LORD M.: Why, only a few weeks ago I started an influential movement to step up the stage censorship. There is altogether too much laxity——

MRS. G.-W.: But you've had your share of triumphs, remember. There were those three publishers and that obscene libel case.

LORD M.: (*cheering up a little*). By George, yes! (*Rises*) That was an achievement of which British Justice can be justly proud. We got 'em twelve months apiece.

MRS. G.-W.: Such respectable men, too. (*Rises.*)

LORD M.: Marriages are breaking up all over the place. Separations are commonplace. In life, in literature and yes—in the drama—adultery is regarded as a jest and divorce as a mere unimportant incident. (*Looking her up and down again.*) There is far too much nonsense talked in this quack kind of

64

psychology.

MRS. G.-W.: (*putting her hand on his arm*). You're so right! What we need is a return to common sense.

LORD M.: (*admiringly*). Gad, Ethel, you haven't changed much.

MRS. G.-W.: Haven't I, Freddie?

LORD M.: As damned attractive as ever. That girl who was in here just now—is she——?

MRS. G.-W.: Yes, Freddie, our daughter. (*To desk*)

LORD M.: Good heavens, what a careless pleasure-loving cad I was.

MRS. G.-W.: Not at all, you were most serious and after all it was hardly your fault.

LORD M.: Of course it was my fault! (*To* C.) Whose fault do you think it was—the Lord Chamberlain's?

MRS. G.-W.: (*to* LORD M.). What I meant was, that the young people nowadays have access to knowledge which was denied to us—knowledge which I believe they take advantage of quite freely.

LORD M.: Please don't mention it to me. (*Sits* R. *of sofa.*)

MRS. G.-W.: Ah, Freddie, what a pity it is that more is not said of—(*sits on sofa*)—the inner and more beautiful side of marriage. Oh, it seems so strange to be sitting beside you again!

LORD M.: Ethel!

MRS. G.-W.: I want to hear about beautiful things
Beautiful things like love
I want to hear about happy marriages
Without complications and just baby carriages
I want to fly to the moon
And hear about June
And dinners at Maxims and Claridges.

I want to hear about beautiful things
Beautiful things like love
I don't want to hear of emotional wrecks
Of people who practise peculiar sex
I want my love to be pure

E   65

My income secure
I don't wish to wallow in a spiritual sewer.

I want to hear about beautiful things
Beautiful things like love
I want to hear the sweet breeze in the trees
I want to hear about the birds but leave out the
    bees.
I don't care if you think it's absurd
If there's never a dirty word
I want to hear only nice things please.

I want to hear about beautiful things
Beautiful things like love
I don't want to know about fornication
But only of people who still keep their station
I want to fly on a cloud
And so to hell with the crowd
I'm content to know the world by inclination
I want to hear about beautiful things.

I want to hear about beautiful things
Beautiful things like love
I want to hear about happy marriages
Without complications and just baby carriages
I want to fly to the moon
And hear about June
And dinners at Maxims and Claridges.

(*They end up on sofa.*)

LORD M.: Ethel, what is it you want out of me? You're not trying to get me to change my will like Evilgreene?

MRS. G.-W.: Is he indeed? In his favour?

LORD M.: More or less, I suppose.

MRS. G.-W.: How can you trust such a man, Freddie? A stranger. What we need, Freddie, is a square deal —Gillian and myself, I mean.

LORD M.: Who? Ah, yes, Gillian. What does your husband

think about Gillian?

MRS. G.-W.: He adores her. Of course he thinks—oh, you've made him very happy, Freddie!

LORD M.: He must be about the only person I have made happy. You know, you're a good woman, Ethel— damn fine woman. I've always thought so. We'll have to see what we can do for you.

MRS. G.-W.: I'm so glad you see my point, Freddie—now don't you think you'd better be getting back?

LORD M.: Yes, perhaps I had. (*They rise.*)

MRS. G.-W.: Now, you must let me help you.

LORD M.: No, it's all right. I feel better. Much better. You've made me feel better, Ethel.

MRS. G.-W.: Have I really, Freddie? You don't know how glad I feel. Shall I help you back to bed?

LORD M.: Yes. Yes. If you would my dear. Looking at you now I feel a new man. Like I was twenty years ago.

MRS. G.-W.: Dear, dear Freddie!
(*They embrace fiercely.*)
Sh! Someone's coming.

LORD M.: By George, Ethel, I'll show the lot of them.
(*He grabs her by the hand and they disappear up the stairs.*)
(DEIRDRE *and* JACK *enter through the panel.*)

DEIRDRE: What about Michael and Lesley? Oh, I think it's disgusting. It isn't love at all, it's an assault course.

JACK: Do you think they saw us?

DEIRDRE: I shouldn't think they could see anyone. Not Michael, certainly. And in the Marsden Room too! Michael of all people—and I thought he was such a bore! How can people deceive you like that?

JACK: And Lesley, too. She seemed to be all woman up there with him. Lesley of all people! That superb creature who stares at you from the pages of glossy magazines. My wife—the new feminine ideal. A long slink of classical meanness. Up

67

there carrying on like Lady Chatterley on ice.

DEIRDRE: Do you think they're suffering?

JACK: Depends what you mean, I suppose.

DEIRDRE: Have they suffered like we have?

JACK: I doubt it. Not Lesley, anyway. She's as tough as a goat.

DEIRDRE: Michael's always been very fond of goats.

JACK: I'm sure Lesley won't want a divorce. If there was a way out I'd take it, believe me.

DEIRDRE: But Jack—darling—I am right, aren't I? We can't go on after what has happened.

(*Enter* GEORGE *to top of stairs with fishing-rod. He is dressed in tweeds.*)

JACK: Yes, you're quite right. Oh, what it must be to be a woman!

DEIRDRE: Oh, that's wonderful! When I think of the easy time you men have compared with the appalling emotional toil that we women——

(*Enter* MICHAEL *and* LESLEY *upstage* L.)

MICHAEL: I say, what's going on?

(JACK *breaks upstage.*)

DEIRDRE: (*very cold*). Jack is complaining that he is worn out with the strain of being a man.

LESLEY: You do surprise me! (*Sits in Gothic chair and leafs through a "Vogue".*)

(*Enter* GILLIAN *upstage* L. *and goes to the desk still with the records.*)

GILLIAN: Do you mind if I play these records in here? That portable in the library sounds dreadful.

MICHAEL: Well, I shouldn't if I were you, my dear. We mustn't forget that his lordship is having a strenuous time of it up there.

(*Enter* LADY MORTLAKE *upstage* L. *with* FATHER EVILGREENE.)

LADY M.: I thought I'd never find a vase. Fortunately Father Evilgreene found one for me. He seems to know where everything is.

FATHER E.: It's time I returned to his lordship. I expect he

68

will be needing me by now. Please excuse me. (*He hands vase to* LADY MORTLAKE.)

(*He smiles at the air above the heads of the company and goes upstairs.*)

(DEIRDRE *crosses and sits on the sofa beside* MICHAEL.)

LADY M.: Ah, well, I'm quite sure Freddie wouldn't want us to sit around being depressed. Why don't we make up a little game of bridge? Would you like to play, Gillian?

GILLIAN: No, thank you.

GEORGE: (*crossing over to* JACK). I happened to overhear what you said just now.

JACK: What?

GEORGE: You know—all that stuff about wishing you were a woman.

JACK: What about it?

GEORGE: (*confidentially*). I have a friend in Harley Street who's made the most extraordinary advances in that kind of thing.

JACK: What kind of thing?

GEORGE: (*rises*) All a matter of injections, dear boy. You must come up to my little lab. Got a whole case of the stuff up there. Just a little stab and phtt! Nearly tried it myself once, but between you and me I've never cared much for the female body. Bit unsightly if you understand me. Can't be compared with—well—mangoes for instance. Ever tried 'em?

JACK: What?

GEORGE: Mangoes.

JACK: What are you talking about?

GEORGE: Oh, you've missed something, believe me. Makes my mouth water just to think of them. Lovely pickled, too. Oh, yes, you must come down with me to the stables sometime. (*To piano and sits on top of it.*)

(*Enter* TREWIN *upstage* L.)

69

TREWIN: (*to* LESLEY). A Mr. Maroon is here asking for you, madam.

GILLIAN: Not Terry Maroon? (*Rises*)

LESLEY: Oh, dear, I suppose he's come down all this way just for me to go through his new number with him. He's quite helpless on his own. Very well, Trewin, you'd better send him in.

LADY M.: Who is Mr. Maroon?

JACK: Terry Maroon is Britain's number one singing star. The new male, tamed and delivered—(*pointing to* LESLEY)—by the new female. He'll come in any moment brushing the floor with his knuckles. (*To* LESLEY.) Is he house-trained too?
(*Enter* TREWIN *with* TERRY MAROON. *Britain's number one singing star needs no description.*)

TREWIN: Mr. Terry Maroon, madam.

TERRY: Hi, everybody!
(*There is a violent crash from upstairs. All turn and look up.*)

MICHAEL: My God!

DEIRDRE: OH! It's the end!

JACK: (*to bottom of stairs*). What is it?

FATHER E.: (*at top window*). His lordship has locked himself in his room.

MICHAEL: We'll come up.

FATHER E.: No, stay where you are!

MRS. G.-W.: (*offstage*). Oh, Freddie!
(*There is a pause, then a mighty noise of splintering wood, a woman's scream and then silence. Presently* FATHER EVILGREENE *returns to the top of the stairs and looks down at them gravely. He nods his head, confirming their fears.*)

GEORGE: What an interesting way to end up—in bed with another man's wife!

(BLACKOUT)

(*End of Scene Eight*)

ACT II

Scene Nine

FATHER EVILGREENE *with small requiem chorus and mourning ballet.*

Throughout his plain number the chorus respond with "You Can't Get Away With It" in the appropriate places.

FATHER E.: What shall be said to the hipsters when they cease, to flip and are silent?
When the false prophets sing no more and lie down with their bankers for ever?
CHORUS: "You Can't Get Away With It."
FATHER E.: What shall be the crazy phrases on the brass plate at the end?
Listen and tremble all you swinging chicks and broads.
CHORUS: "You Can't Get Away With It."
FATHER E.: When the last flip comes who shall be hip still?
They who are hung up now shall not hang on when the time comes.
It will surely bug you when there is no man to hug, and no tea to push. There shall be no Zen to the left of you nor throne to the right of you.
CHORUS: "You Can't Get Away With It."
FATHER E.: Death is a round hole which hath no place for squares.
Then you will go, man, truly you will go, and you will be bugged for ever.
CHORUS: "You Can't Get Away With It."
FATHER E.: For this is the swinging truth. If you dig all things, you shall reap no harvest.
For this is the crazy truth. You can't get away

71

with it.

For this is the swinging truth. If you dig all things, you will reap nothing at the end.

(*Mourning ballet, with the family, dancers and* JO)

(BLACKOUT)

(*End of Scene Nine*)

ACT II

Scene Ten

LADY MORTLAKE *is seated at her desk, replying to her correspon-dence on black-edged notepaper. From the hall outside comes the sound of* TERRY *softly singing his latest hit.* DEIRDRE *is leaning against a chair, her back to the audience.*

DEIRDRE: I'm sorry, Mummy, but I'm afraid I just can't believe in a God any longer. When you find yourself called upon to pay tax at nineteen and sixpence in the pound, the idea of a Divine Providence suddenly seems rather laughable. And how much longer is Father Evilgreene going to stay here?

LADY M.: Oh, he's leaving to take up some appointment tomorrow.

DEIRDRE: I'm sure he put Daddy up to making that utterly stupid will.

LADY M.: I don't see why you should call it utterly stupid, Deirdre. It merely says that the income will be stopped, and diverted to a suitable charity of Father Evilgreene's choice——

DEIRDRE: We all know the name of that charity!

LADY M.: If either you or Lesley should divorce your husbands, or vice versa. I don't see how it can affect either of you. It's simply a moral precaution. I expect your father was anxious to protect you both. It's so like him. Poor, dear Freddie!

DEIRDRE: It seems to me that Daddy had a genius for finding reasons for not doing things.

LADY M.: Of course, dear. That is the very basis of all religions and no one understood it better than your father.

73

DEIRDRE: Oh, Mummy, how can you be so calm! What are you doing, anyway?

LADY M.: I am replying to Lady Bartlett's letter of sympathy. I have also told her that she can, of course, still depend on my assistance with next month's hunt ball.

DEIRDRE: You're still going!

LADY M.: Most certainly. The everyday business of living must go on just the same, Deirdre—Freddie would have wished that.

DEIRDRE: It isn't as though we shall even be able to afford to hunt any more.

LADY M.: I think we have all learned to rough it in the last few years, and it should stand us in good stead. Anyway, we need not give up hunting altogether. It's a democratic sport, above all things—we can still follow in the car. Oh, we'll manage somehow, my dear. Thank goodness Mrs. Giltedge-Whyte has agreed to pay twice my usual fee for sponsoring young Gillian!

DEIRDRE: It's about the least she could do, in the circumstances.

LADY M.: You must curb that tongue of yours, Deirdre. Father Evilgreene assures me that when he went into your father's room, she was merely helping him back into bed.

DEIRDRE: "Any charity of his choice"!

LADY M.: As both you and Lesley are quite happily married, I really don't see that there's any harm done. (*Enter* JACK.)

DEIRDRE: Where have you been?

JACK: Oh, trying to work things out.

DEIRDRE: I know. So have I.

LADY M.: Well, I must leave you children to yourselves. I haven't seen George since the funeral. I do hope he isn't up to something. (*Exit.*)

DEIRDRE: But what are we going to do about it? We can't get married. For one thing, I know that Michael would never agree to a divorce. He's too much like Daddy for that. Besides, he's got his beastly career to consider, apart from the money.

JACK: Lesley wouldn't agree either. She's too mean to give up your dad's money, anyway.

DEIRDRE: How could Daddy be so cruel!

JACK: And when I think of all the money she's making out of that lout in there! Listen to him! (*Indicating the direction of* TERRY'S *voice*.)

(*Enter* LESLEY *and* MICHAEL.)

LESLEY: I can't think why you should object. At least it saves you from having to buy your wife's clothes. And I have such expensive tastes. Most men would be delighted, I'm sure. Wouldn't you, Michael?

MICHAEL: Why yes, I suppose so.

JACK: Listen to that timid, emasculated male!

MICHAEL: Now look here, you be careful what you say!

JACK: We're all being slowly deflowered—deflowered by the female!

DEIRDRE: Deflowered! Honestly, Jack you do exaggerate!

JACK: Oh, no I don't.

MICHAEL: Come, my dear fellow, this is no way to talk to the ladies.

JACK: (*as* TERRY *reaches a crescendo*). Do you hear that nasal blubbering about little flowers and watching new-born babies cry? Of loving you, and no one but you? Baby, you're all mine, all mine through all eternity? That so-called man in there is making two thousand pounds a week—thanks to my wife— for what? For emptying the slop buckets of modern love into a microphone, for crawling and cringing before the almighty tyranny of the bosom.

MICHAEL: I say . . .

JACK: . . . for moaning his snivelling hymns to the female figure.

DEIRDRE: Do you mean to say that you don't believe in— well, love, any more?

75

JACK: No, Deirdre—this has nothing to do with you and me.

DEIRDRE: Of course it has everything to do with you and me! Oh, Jack, how could you!

JACK: Oh, for heaven's sake, Deirdre, don't take all I say personally!

(*As he shouts at her irritably, her face puckers slowly into tears.*)

There's no reason why it should affect you and me. I'll tell you we'll work it out somehow.

DEIRDRE: How can we possibly work it out! I think I could die!

JACK: All this business has upset my system.

LESLEY: His masculine sensitivity he means.

DEIRDRE: My poor darling! Put your head in my lap.

(*He does so gratefully.*)

There! (*And she strokes his forehead tenderly.*)

LESLEY: You see—there are still some of the old-fashioned kind of women left around. Poor Jack thinks I'm cold, don't you, darling?

JACK: (*viciously*). You're like the school lavatory seat in December!

MICHAEL: Oakham, only a cad would say a thing like that to a lady! Get up!

DEIRDRE: Leave him alone, you bully!

MICHAEL: Well, really!

DEIRDRE: (*threateningly*). Do you want a black eye?

MICHAEL: Well, I'm dashed if I really know what this is all about. I'm just a plain, ordinary chap, as you all know, and it seems to me that we have a jolly ticklish situation here. Damn it all, Oakham, let's be frank. It's bad enough just one of us carrying on with the other's wife, but both of us doing it is pretty damned indecent. I'm not a prig, I hope, but I have to say that I'm shocked. Yes, shocked!

JACK: I suppose you don't want to marry my wife, by any chance?

MICHAEL: Lesley and I have discussed the matter, and we

have both decided against it. Lesley feels that my own career would clash with hers, and I respect her point of view. After all, she is a highly accomplished woman, and we must recognize the fact that woman—ah—is taking a new place in our rapidly changing society. We men will have to review our position, and—ah—bring it into line with present-day developments.

DEIRDRE: I shall have to do him soon.

MICHAEL: As far as this question . . .

(*Enter* GEORGE, *carrying a small leather bag. He stares at the company, particularly at* JACK *with his head still in* DEIRDRE'S *lap. He starts to go up the stairs.*)

GEORGE: (*to* LESLEY). Shan't be long.

LESLEY: All right, George.

(*Exit* GEORGE)

I believe there may be a solution to all this.

DEIRDRE: Meaning?

LESLEY: Michael and I have just seen something very remarkable, haven't we, Michael?

MICHAEL: What? Oh yes, indeed. Most extraordinary!

LESLEY: George has just taken us down to the stables.

DEIRDRE: Well?

LESLEY: It seems that George is really on to something pretty important. So important that it takes one's breath away.

DEIRDRE: What is it, for heaven's sake?

LESLEY: You know Robert?

JACK: The hunter? I know that vicious devil all right!

LESLEY: Well, the vicious devil is as gentle as a lamb, and from now on, it looks as though we'll have to call him Roberta.

DEIRDRE: Roberta? What *do* you mean?

LESLEY: I mean that old Robert has become a rather flirtatious mare, and that your mare, Christine, has become a particularly overpowering stallion.

DEIRDRE: I don't believe it!

77

JACK: Well, I do. George is capable of anything. He should be in Ealing Films.

LESLEY: Quite briefly, they have both changed their sex. Isn't that correct, Michael?

MICHAEL: Yes, it's quite correct, Deirdre. I couldn't believe my eyes—but there it was.

DEIRDRE: But how did it happen?

JACK: Was it this injection he was talking about?

LESLEY: It was. And we both watched him administer it.

MICHAEL: No question of trickery, I assure you. I don't think I'm easily taken in by these things, and I watched very closely indeed.

LESLEY: It was staggering.

MICHAEL: Bit embarrassing, too.

LESLEY: Staggering and most exciting!

JACK: But how did they react? Wasn't there any discomfort?

LESLEY: None at all. Whole thing took a matter of minutes. I tell you, it's revolutionary! Just think of it! After all, it had to come sooner or later. We all know that the line dividing male and female is little more than a vague shadow.

DEIRDRE: Personally, I've always found it rather obvious. Am I being terribly old-fashioned?

LESLEY: Now George has got enough of this stuff up in that little room of his to enter all this year's Derby runners for the Oaks as well.

DEIRDRE: Poor Christine! Well, I think it's disgusting.

LESLEY: Do you? I'm sure Jack doesn't agree with you.

JACK: What are you getting at?

LESLEY: I should have thought it was plain. If men have become sloppy, boneless and emasculated, it's their own fault entirely.

MICHAEL: I say, it is a bit strong, old girl! I never thought for a moment that you felt like that about us chaps. I mean, then—well, why did you——

LESLEY: Have an affair with you, Michael? Because, my dear, I still have a great many instincts of the

78

purely biological female.

MICHAEL: Ah—yes. Quite.

DEIRDRE: I want to know what you are leading up to.

LESLEY: Simply this. Firstly, we are all, I think, what might be described fairly accurately as maladjusted.

MICHAEL: Good heavens! You don't mean that we're not—normal!

LESLEY: You're a politician, Michael, and what you want, therefore, is power. And power, political power, like everything else, is passing into the hands of the women. Look to the future, Michael. Don't fight new battles with an old weapon! If you want to make certain of being a success in politics, there is only one realistic solution: become a woman!

MICHAEL: Lesley! You don't mean change our sex!

LESLEY: Certainly.

MICHAEL: (*appealing to the others*). I don't know what you think, but that seems a pretty insulting thing to say to a chap. Why, if another chap made a suggestion like that to me, I'd knock him down!

JACK: Quite right—punch him on the nose!

MICHAEL: I'm not a fool, you know—I've been in the Army!

LESLEY: Don't you see, Michael, if you and Jack were to change your sex, your marriages would be naturally annulled. You would be free to do as you like—and without losing any money by having to go through with a divorce.

MICHAEL: I suppose you make it sound pretty plausible, Lesley. I can only say this—I shall give it my earnest attention. I can't say any more than that at the moment.

LESLEY: You could make the change as often as you liked. You could be a woman all the week, and a man at the weekends, for instance.

DEIRDRE: No, if he marries me, he won't!

JACK: Or a woman at the weekend and a man all the week. A—

woman at the weekend and a man all the week

79

	Two days as Madame Pompadour and five as an Ancient Greek.
	You could swop your pretty bras
	For a moustache with handlebars
	And be a woman at the weekend and a man all the week.
ALL:	A woman at the weekend and a man all the week.
JACK AND LESLEY:	We could start the most exciting and exclusive clique.
MICHAEL AND DEIRDRE:	If we're too tired when to go to bed
	We could change our trews instead
	And be a woman at the weekend and a man all the week.
ALL:	A woman at the weekend and a man all the week.
DEIRDRE:	The thought of putting horrid shaving lotion on my cheek
	Of giving up my perfume by Dior
	For some stuff called "Saddle Sore",
	I think it's positively ghastly—all this sexual hide and seek!
	(*To* JACK.) I suppose *you* like the idea?
JACK:	What?
DEIRDRE:	Well, of being a woman at the weekend
ALL:	. . . and a man all the week!
LESLEY:	Broad shouldered and belligerent
JACK AND MICHAEL:	With curves and furs and Cadillacs to keep us meek.
LESLEY AND DEIRDRE:	You would never have the fag
	Of dressing up in drag
	You'd be a woman at the weekend.
JACK AND MICHAEL:	. . . and a man all the week!
ALL:	A woman at the weekend and a man all the week
	We'd all know what's what—we'd have had our weekly peek

From our heads to our toes
We'd give seven different shows
As a woman at the weekend and a man all the
week!
All the week! All the week!
(*They end up with* JACK *and* MICHAEL *sitting on the
sofa,* DEIRDRE *perched on its downstage arm, and*
LESLEY *sitting in the Gothic chair.*)

LESLEY: Well, what do you say?

JACK: And what about you?

LESLEY: Me?

JACK: (*goes to* LESLEY). Yes, you. Are you as anxious as
I am to discontinue our association?

LESLEY: (*goes to sofa*). Well, darling, you must admit it is
getting rather dreary, isn't it?

JACK: Look, I'll tell you what I'll do. I'll agree to this.
(*Goes to stairs.*)

MICHAEL: What!

DEIRDRE: (*runs over to* JACK, *then downstage to chair*). You're
mad! Darling, think of your manhood!

JACK: I have. But I'll do it under one condition.

LESLEY: (*goes to stairs*). And that is!

JACK: That if I go upstairs to George's room, you'll
come up and have a jab of the old hypodermic at
the same time. Different mixture, of course.

LESLEY: I see.

JACK: Well, what do you say? Aren't you raring to let
that inner man of yours get going?

LESLEY: I must admit it would be rather a relief. Very well,
I'll try it.

JACK: When?

LESLEY: Whenever you like.

JACK: Right—let's go. We can swop clothes in my room.

DEIRDRE: Jack, don't! I don't trust it! I think the whole
thing is phoney.

JACK: Now don't worry, darling.
(*They embrace, downstage of the Gothic chair.*)
Everything's going to be all right.

DEIRDRE: (*running her hands over his chest*). But when I think
of it! Oh, it's awful! You can't do this to me,
Jack. Why, we shan't be able to——

JACK: Sh! Deirdre, darling. I've made up my mind. I'm
doing this for us. I'm tired of this miserable stupid
life we've been leading. At last, there's a way out.

DEIRDRE: (*feeling under his shirt*). Oh, he won't even have
lovely hair on his chest any more! Jack! If you
love me, you won't do this!

JACK: Darling, it's because I love you that I'm doing it.
Everything will be all right, I promise you.
(*He kisses her.*)

DEIRDRE: But I'd even bought socks for your birthday!
What can I do with them?

JACK: Give them to Lesley. (*Goes to stairs.*) I tell you
what you can do—ring FLE 10,000. Well, Michael,
have you made up your mind yet?

MICHAEL: I—er—don't think I am prepared to make a
statement just at present. Bit overwhelmed, you
know. I shall wait and watch—ah—further
developments before I commit myself to any
course of policy. This has made me uneasy. Yes,
very uneasy. Well, good luck, old chap.
(*They shake hands on the stairs, and* DEIRDRE
collapses into tears.)

MICHAEL: (*to* LESLEY). Good luck, old girl!

LESLEY: Thank you, Michael.

MICHAEL: (*eyes her delightful figure doubtfully*). Sure you're
doing the right thing, old girl!
(*She nods and smiles, then turns to* JACK, *and they
run upstairs together, leaving* MICHAEL *to flap and*
DEIRDRE *to wail on the sofa.*)

DEIRDRE: (*pounding the sofa*). How could he do this to me!

MICHAEL: Try not to take it too much to heart, my dear.

DEIRDRE: (*hysterical*). Oh, Michael, do try not to be such a
fool! It wouldn't matter if you were to change
your sex!
(*She crosses to the door upstage* L., *as* TERRY *and*

82

GILLIAN *enter, hand-in-hand.*)

Nobody would care. Oh, I shall never forgive
him! (*Pushing them aside*) Oh, get out of my way!
(*Exits through upstage* L. *arch.*)

TERRY: Is she upset about something? (*Goes to* C.)

MICHAEL: Ah-yes. I'm afraid she is rather.

TERRY: Anything I can do to help?

MICHAEL: I think not, thank you.

TERRY: After all, that's what we're here for, isn't it?

MICHAEL: I beg your pardon?

TERRY: Why, helping each other along life's way.

MICHAEL: Yes. I suppose you're right.

TERRY: If you bring a little smile along, you can't go
wrong.

(*He and* GILLIAN *rub their cheeks together.*)

MICHAEL: Well, if you will excuse me . . .

TERRY: We're not driving you out, are we?

MICHAEL: Not at all. I must go for a walk, that's all. I have
rather a difficult problem on my mind.

TERRY: O.K. Mike. You go for your walk. And maybe
when you come back, you'd like to talk about it.

MICHAEL: Thank you very much.

TERRY: After all, if we can share our troubles—that's
right, isn't it, darling?

GILLIAN: Yes, darling.

(*They kiss lingeringly, their foreheads touching,
still holding hands, and sit on the sofa.*)

MICHAEL: She may be right at that! She may be right!
(*He turns to go out, and bumps into* MRS.
GILTEDGE-WHYTE *coming in through the arch upstage*
R.)

MRS. G.-W.: Ah, Mr. Rawley. Have you seen my daughter,
Gillian?

MICHAEL: Please excuse me—I'm in a hurry.
(*Exit upstage* R.)

MRS. G.-W.: Oh! (*Calls out after him.*) I advise you to be very
careful if you go down to the paddock. There are
two very peculiar horses down there. (*To herself*)

83

Well, I do hope that they won't do him an injury, that's all. (*Comes downstage, and suddenly sees* TERRY *and* GILLIAN *head to head.*) Gillian! What are you doing? (*To sofa.*)

GILLIAN: I should have thought it was obvious, Mummy. (TERRY *rises.*)
Terry and I are in love, Mummy.

MRS. G.-W.: I see. Is this true, Mr. Maroon?

GILLIAN: Now, please, Mummy, don't——

MRS. G.-W.: Just a moment, Gillian. I am speaking to Mr. Maroon.

TERRY: Yes, Mrs. Giltedge-Whyte. I guess it's true, all right. Gillian and me really love each other.

GILLIAN: And we want to get married.

MRS. G.-W.: I hope you haven't tried to seduce my daughter, Mr. Maroon!

GILLIAN: Oh, Mummy, you are the end! (*Flounces to* L.)

TERRY: (*embarrassed*). Honestly, Mrs. Giltedge-Whyte, such an idea never entered my head. You see, I was brought up to respect women, and I do, I really do. You know something? I believe that the greatest thing in this world of ours is the love between a man and a woman.
(*Overcome at this sentiment,* MRS. GILTEDGE-WHYTE *feels her way to the Gothic chair.*)

MRS. G.-W.: Really? Is that why you sing as you do? (*Sits*)

TERRY: But certainly. Why, you've just got to be sincere in my business, Mrs. Giltedge-Whyte. They'd spot it in a moment if I wasn't. Why, when I sing to all those millions of simple, ordinary little people—folks like you and me, Mrs. Giltedge-Whyte—
(MRS. GILTEDGE-WHYTE *swallows bravely.*)
—they know I'm singing to each one of them personally, and that's why they write to me and tell me their little personal problems. You see, I speak a kind of language that everyone can understand.
(*Enter* LESLEY *at the head of the stairs, dressed in*

JACK'S *clothes, a transformed vision of emancipated masculinity, and smoking a cigar.*)

LESLEY: Excuse me, but have any of you seen Mr. Rawley?

MRS. G.-W.: Why, yes. He went out there just a few minutes ago, Mr.——?

LESLEY: Please excuse me. I'm afraid I can't introduce myself just for a moment. (*Strides out through the upstage arch.*)

GILLIAN: What an attractive man!

MRS. G.-W.: He seemed like most young men nowadays to me —rather effeminate. How different they were in Lord Mortlake's time—and your father's of course. (*Turning back to* TERRY) You were saying?

TERRY: Well, I was just saying that I'll dedicate my life to Gillian.

I'll see that the stars shine in her eyes,
I'll be certain her life will be one long surprise,
And before I make a pass
(TREWIN *enters upstage* L. *with a practical hand microphone on a silver salver, which he presents to* TERRY.)
I'll tell her that the sun shines out of her face.
This isn't any madam,
I've known lots of girls before,
And, frankly, I've had 'em.

I'm hers, all hers,
From here to eternity,
I'll dedicate my life to my pretty little wife,
And hand in hand,
Through love's wonderland,
I'll be hers.
(*Throughout this interchange he holds the microphone in front of whoever is talking.*)

MRS. G.-W.: Quite! And do you feel you can offer Gillian the kind of life she's been accustomed to?
After all——

TERRY: Oh! I'm not worthy of her. I realize that!

85

MRS. G.-W.: Oh! You do?

TERRY: I look at her and I know I am just a piece of dirt —just a little old piece of dirt beneath her pretty feet.

MRS. G.-W.: You certainly seem to be entering on the idea of marriage with the right attitude, Mr. Maroon.

TERRY: I'm hers, all hers,
In health and maternity.
At night we'll get undressed
In our lovely little nest,
And in a year or two,
We'll have a little kid like you,
Which will be hers.

Even when her hair's in curls,
I won't sleep with other girls,
I'm going to be true
Because she'll look like you,
(*Points to* MRS. GILTEDGE-WHYTE.)
I'm hers, all hers,
I don't want to belong to me,
All my life it's my choice,

GILLIAN: Terry, darling!

TERRY: To be waked up by that voice,
She'll drive me insane,
My sweet, gold ball-and-chain,
I'll be hers, hers,
My love, my high life,
My posh trouble-and-strife,
I'll be hers.
(*Takes a running jump off the sofa and lands kneeling downstage* C.)
(TREWIN *re-enters from upstage* L. *with the salver and takes the microphone from* TERRY.)

TREWIN: (*speaking into microphone*). Thank you, sir.

MRS. G.-W.: Now, Mr.—er?

TERRY: Call me Terry, please. All my fans do. (*Goes to* MRS. GILTEDGE-WHYTE.)

86

MRS. G.-W.: Er—Terry. Are you an American?

TERRY: Blimey—no! What made you think that?

MRS. G.-W.: I find it rather difficult to follow you, that's all.

TERRY: Nice of you to think so, anyway. Thanks very much. It's the clothes, I guess.

(*Enter* JACK *at the head of the stairs, dressed in* LESLEY'S *clothes, and in what looks suspiciously like a wig.*)

JACK: Excuse me, but have you seen Deirdre? (*Taps* TERRY *playfully on the shoulder.*)

TERRY: Yeah. She went that way, Miss—— (*Points off upstage* L.)

JACK: (*exiting as quickly as he can*). Oh, thank you so much.

MRS. G.-W.: Excuse me, but you are remarkably like Mr. Oakham.

JACK: Yes, I'm his sister, Jack—Jacqueline! Please forgive me, I have to be running along now! (*Exit upstage* L.)

MRS. G.-W.: It's all very extraordinary. I don't believe any of it.

TERRY: She's quite a smasher, isn't she?

MRS. G.-W.: Who?

TERRY: This Jacqueline.

MRS. G.-W.: I really couldn't say. Young girls nowadays are so busy trying to look like men, with their short hair and tight trousers, it's almost impossible to judge them by the standards that were accepted when I was a girl. You were saying?

TERRY: (*to sofa*). Well, as for looking after Gillian, you needn't have any worries about that.

MRS. G.-W.: Yes, yes! How much *do* you make?

TERRY: (*Sits on sofa.*) Well, there's a thousand pounds a week from record sales alone. With the rest, radio. TV., the halls—well, it ain't peanuts, Mrs. Giltedge-Whyte.

MRS. G.-W.: No, I'm sure it isn't.

TERRY: Of course, Mrs. Oakham—she's my manager— she handles all the financial side. Do you know,

MRS. G.-W.: she taught me how to sing?

MRS. G.-W.: Did she? (*Crosses to sofa.*)

TERRY: Oh, yes. I was just the lift boy in her bra factory you see. Well, one day I was taking her up in the lift, and she hears me singing and there I was! And you know why she believed in me?

MRS. G.-W.: I've no idea. (*Sits on sofa.*)

TERRY: Because I was sincere. Why, look at this suit I'm wearing. How much do you think it cost? No— go on, feel that material. How much do you think? Have a guess! No idea? Forty-eight quid! You don't think I get that being insincere? Believe me, Gillian will have the very best—you can bet your drawers on that! (*Goes to* GILLIAN.) And don't think I won't look after her old mum too. Look after my own mum—so why not Gillian's? Well, what do you say, Mum? (*Puts his arm round* GILLIAN.)

MRS. G.-W.: Well, I must admit, Terry, that you have impressed me enormously with your sincerity. I can only say that it's a great pity there are not more young men with your serious, responsible attitude to life.

TERRY: Oh, I'm serious, all right. (*To* GILLIAN) Aren't I, baby?

MRS. G.-W.: I think you are something of a poet. Yes, you are a true poet of the age we live in, a guardian of the *status quo*, of morality, and yes, of religion, too.

TERRY: But honestly, Mum, how can I help it? Why, every time I hear a new-born baby cry——

GILLIAN: Oh, not now, darling.

MRS. G.-W.: What a sweet boy you are! Quite charming. Yes, you can certainly have my blessing.

TERRY: Good old Mum! (*Hugging her*)

GILLIAN: Mummy, you are sweet, really. I knew you'd just adore him! (*Hugs her.*)

MRS. G.-W.: This means, of course, Gillian, that we shall have to cancel all the arrangements I made with Lady Mortlake. I must remember to stop that cheque, too.

(*Enter* JACK *through the arch upstage* L., *panting*.)
Why, what's the matter? Is somebody chasing you?
(*He nods*.)

TERRY: Has somebody tried to molest you, miss?

JACK: I'm afraid so.

TERRY: O.K. Where is he?

JACK: No, please don't bother. It doesn't matter. Oh!
(*Suddenly the eager figure of* FATHER EVILGREENE
hurtles on in hot pursuit. He puts his hand out to
JACK *when he sees the others*.)

FATHER E.: Ah! This young lady and I were having a little
theological discussion. I'm sorry if we disturbed
you. (*To* JACK) Coming, my dear?

MRS. G.-W.: Just one moment, sir. I have been trying to place
your face ever since I arrived. I believe you're an
imposter. Are you not the Father Evilgreene who
ran a disreputable school in Ponders End until you
were exposed in the Sunday newspapers last year?
(FATHER EVILGREENE *stares at her, and then makes
a quick dash for the door. But* TERRY *is there first
and knocks him down*.)

GILLIAN: Terry! I didn't know you were so strong!

TERRY: Don't worry, honey. He won't get away.
(*Enter* LESLEY *and* DEIRDRE, *arm-in-arm, from the
arch upstage* R.)

JACK: Deirdre! There you are! I've been looking for you
all over the place.

DEIRDRE: It's no good, Jack. It's all over between us.
Besides, I've found Lesley now.

JACK: You found Lesley? You really went ahead with all
this?

LESLEY: Of course, didn't you?

JACK: (*pulling off his wig*). No, of course not. You mean
you want that instead of me?

DEIRDRE: Exactly. We've found each other, haven't we,
darling?

LESLEY: That's right. (*They cross to piano*.)

(GEORGE *appears at the window, with his trout bag, grinning.*)

GEORGE: Trout are rising this evening.

JACK: Shut up! This is your fault!

(*Enter* LADY MORTLAKE *through upstage* R. *arch with an enormous bunch of flowers.*)

LADY M.: Ah! Here we all are! Dear me, Father Evilgreene what are you doing down there? Not still praying? Well, now, I'm just wondering what I should do with these.

JACK: I can't believe it! I can't believe it! Oh, woman, you are the devil's doorway all right!

(MICHAEL *staggers in from the upstage* R. *arch, looking a mild wreck.*)

And what's the matter with you?

MICHAEL: That bloody horse! I can't tell you what it's done to me! Anyway, I've settled his little game once and for all. (*His voice breaks into a high squeak.*) George!

(*Enter* TREWIN *upstage* L.)

LADY M.: What is it, Trewin?

TREWIN: Some gentlemen in an 'elicopter, my lady.

LADY M.: An 'elicopter? What's that?

TREWIN: It's landed on the front lawn, my lady. They say they're from *The Daily Racket*—Mr. Paul Slickey's column.

JACK: (*wildly*). By God, yes! Why don't we give the entire Paul Slickey office a shot. Bring your little black bag down here.

MICHAEL: Yes, I say, George!

(GEORGE *grins down at them and disappears.* JACK *dashes up the stairs after him.*)

George! Come back with that stuff! George! You little bastard!

(MICHAEL *crawls up after him.*)

MICHAEL: (*feebly*). George! I say, George!

LADY M.: Do give Father Evilgreene a hand, Terry. He looks so miserable down there. And why don't you sing us one of your nice songs?

MRS. G.-W.: Oh, yes, What a good idea!

(TERRY *ignores* FATHER EVILGREENE *who is still nursing his nose, and runs over to stairs.*)

TERRY: O.K. everybody! Let's go! (*To* MRS. GILTEDGE-WHYTE) After you, Mum.

(*She comes downstage and the Mortlake gauze drops in behind her.*)

MRS. G.-W.:   I want to hear about beautiful things,
Beautiful things like love.
I don't want to hear of emotional wrecks.
Of people who practise peculiar sex.
I want my love to be pure—my income secure,
I don't want to wallow in a spiritual sewer.

I want to hear about beautiful things
Beautiful things like love.
I want to hear about happy marriages
Without complications and just baby carriages,
I want to fly to the moon—and hear about June,
And dinners at Maxims and Claridges.

(*Exits downstage* L.)

(BLACKOUT)

(*Mortlake gauze goes away.*)

91

ACT II

Scene Eleven

"The Daily Racket".
JACK *at his desk in his shirtsleeves, alone.*

JACK: That's another one to bed!
    (*Enter* SECRETARY.)
JO: Did you call, darling?
JACK: No, but I'm afraid I would have done later.
    (*They embrace.*)
    What have we got in for tomorrow?
    (*She shows him the papers.*)
    People, more people! More flesh and blood, more
    human interest! More of the truth about the world
    in which we all live, the people, the ordinary people!
    (*He grabs her.*)
    My God! What a function we fulfil!
    What a service we dispense! Nothing too trivial or
    unimportant for us to package up for
    consumption at the breakfast table or on the
    eight-fifteen! Just think of our circulation figures,
    the multitudes who hunger and yet starve not!
    And why? Because of us, of us! This happy breed
    of men who give them what they want! (*Hurling
    papers in the air.*) These are our loaves and fishes!
    Come, come and pay your tuppence-halfpenny and
    let no man be turned away or unregarded! *We* have
    food for all. What's on tomorrow?
JO: Well, a new night club opened tonight. You might
    still catch a bit of it.
JACK: Good! I'm hungry. Give me my jacket. What else?

92

JO: In the morning there's a meeting of nuclear
scientists who want to end war.

JACK: Communists and queers!

JO: Then at twelve o'clock there's a Press reception at
the Dorchester to launch a new British film.

JACK: Whores and longhairs! Still, I'll be thirsty by then.
Hand me my hat.

JO: Then there is an interview with Dominique Flanders,
the distinguished poet and Nobel Prize winner.
(*Fetches hat and rose.*)

JACK: That phoney!

JO: Then London Airport to meet Red Evans, the film
star.

JACK: Think of all the money he must make! What's he
got that's so special? Why do I have to go and
meet his lousy plane and look at his beautiful
hand-made shoes? Why is there no justice in this
world?

JO: (*putting his hat on his head*). Darling, that's not
your department.

JACK: Sure. It's a racket. (*Kisses her.*) Just another
racket.

(JOURNALISTS *enter.*)

JO: Match your poor seductiveness against this
goddam bitch success.
You may not have prowess but who's the hell
to guess,
As long as somehow you progress, we'll give
you happiness.
You've got to understand the mechanics of
success.

JACK: (*stands on desk*).
If I could be an M.P.
Part of Democracy,
Whatever I said,
You could take it as read,
Whitehall gives the orders—it
Wouldn't be me!

93

If I could be a lifetime Peer,
You'd have nothing to fear,
I'd beat up the whores
Keep them working indoors,
For the sake of the kiddies we'd have
English veneer.

JO AND JOURNALISTS:

You've got to understand the mechanics of
success, *etc.*

JACK: If I could be a magistrate,
You'd have to be importunate,
With the police on all fours
It's their word—not yours!
If you're up before me—it would be
Unfortunate! (*Falls into dancer's arms.*)

If I could live in Downing Street,
On the telly I'd look a treat.
If Ike went to hell,
Then I'd go as well
And I'd bring you lot with me—and
We'd all lick his feet!

JO AND JOURNALISTS:

You've got to understand the mechanics of
success, *etc.*

JACK: If I could be a soldier man,
Shooting up black men whenever I can,
I won't fight real battles,
In case Randolph tattles,
I'm not only strong, I'm antediluvian!

If I could build a rocket base,
I'd be a copper and smash in your face.
I'd wield all officialdom's might
If you'd dare to interfere with our right
To blow all you bleeders to outer space.

JO AND JOURNALISTS:

You've got to understand the mechanics of

success, *etc.*

A REPORTER: (*comes to* JACK). Who did you say you were?

> (JACK *puts his hat on the reporter's head, his holder in his mouth.* JO *puts* JACK'S *coat on the reporter.* JACK *exits* R., *disgusted, while* JO *throws the rose down.*)

JO AND JOURNALISTS:

> If you're going to impress, you must pander to the Press,
> They'll want you to assess how much money you possess.
> You've got to understand the mechanics of success.
>
> (*The Keyhole drops in behind the other "Slickey". He turns to face the audience.*)

REPORTER:
> I'm just a guy called Paul Slickey
> And the job that I do's pretty tricky.
> I'm twenty-eight years old.
>
> (*The* COMPANY *come downstairs; the Keyhole has flown away. The principals all have boards which they show the audience and then take their places in the line-up.*)

FULL COMPANY:
> And practically everybody, anybody, anything you can think of
> Leaves me quite completely
> Newspaper neatly
> Quite, quite cold.
>
> Don't think you can fool a guy like him
> The best things in life are never free
> Guys like him who are on the inside
> Cannot be taken for a ride,
> He has professional ways and means
> Of getting in behind the scenes
> To put the screws on stars in jeans
> They don't need hidden television screens.
>
> He'll be always on the band waggon, never in

95